GARDEN OF THE BRAVE IN WAR

GARDEN OF
THE BRAVE
IN WAR

Recollections of Iran

TERENCE O'DONNELL

The University of Chicago Press

Chicago & London

The University of Chicago Press, Chicago 60637
The University of Chicago Press, Ltd., London

"The Trip for Wood" and "The Pilgrimage" previously appeared in
somewhat different form in *The Atlantic Monthly*.

Library of Congress Cataloging in Publication Data

O'Donnell, Terence.
    Garden of the brave in war : recollections of Iran / Terence
  O'Donnell. — University of Chicago Press ed.
        p.   cm.
    Originally published: New Haven, Conn. : Ticknor & Fields, 1980.
  1. Iran—Description and travel.   2. Iran—Social life and
customs.   1. Title.
DS259.036   1988
955—dc19
ISBN 0−226−61764−5 (pbk.)   87−30068
                                                  CIP

To the memory of Richard Weaver
of the University of Chicago 1944–1963

and for Julian Bach
and
Chester and Joan Kerr

Contents

Most of the names of people in this book have been changed.

Preface

In the early 1960s I went to live on a farm in Persia — or Iran, as it is now more usually called — and remained for nearly a decade. While there I kept a journal, and it is on that journal that this book is based. The journal entries which follow are selected from it, while the stories relate, often verbatim, events and people contained in it.

In this journal I wrote about a variety of subjects, with one deliberate exception — politics. This was partly because, as a foreigner in the country, I did not think that politics were any of my concern. I had known too many Americans playing like boys with political fire in societies they did not understand. Also, I have always tended to view politics as one of society's more unfortunate excrescences, one which distracts the observer from an understanding of a society's true nature. This is, of course, a bitter and fallacious view. Obviously politics is one reflection of a people's character. Therefore, insofar as this book is about Iranian character — and to a considerable degree it is — it does pertain here and there to the recent turmoil in Iran.

For example, after reading this book, no one should be surprised that the Iranian Revolution took a religious form. The fact that God appears on almost every page does not reflect religious convictions of my own, nor for that matter any conscious design at all, but simply arises from the circumstance that in any description of the fabric of Iranian life God is an endlessly repeated motif.

There are other motifs as well that appear both in these pages and in recent reports on Iran. For example, that strongly individualistic, indeed anarchical, strain in the Iranian character which so often prevents sustained cooperation. There is, too, the readiness to engage in revenge and to relish it. Also, capriciousness and sudden shifts in feeling. Outbreaks of violence in a sometimes very vicious form. Deviousness and the conviction that all others are devious too. There are as well, in these pages and in recent happenings, certain other qualities of character which in the circumstances of the revolution tended to go unreported: Iranian compassion, tenderness, and generosity, their humor and playfulness. Humor and playfulness may seem at odds with the grisly happenings of the revolution, but Iranians are like all old peoples who have known centuries of turmoil and tragedy: one of their answers to the death's-head has been laughter and dalliance.

There are two motifs in the revolution that decidedly do not appear in these pages for the reason that they are so uncommon as to be aberrations. One is puritanism, by which I mean the puritanism of the religious regimen. Iranians are voluptuaries and delight in the flesh. Their conversation, their poetry — which means everything to them after their God, and sometimes before — their folklore, and their traditions — all reflect a love of earthly pleasures. The execution of prostitutes following the revolution could only have horrified the ordinary, susceptible, forgiving Iranian heart.

The second aberration, a cousin to the first, is fanaticism. From the beginnings of Iranian history, from the times of Cyrus, toleration has again and again been the hallmark of the Iranian state and also one of the most pronounced and common traits in the individual Iranian. Nonetheless, and however much an aberration, fanaticism certainly played a part in the revolution. Perhaps revolutions cannot take place without it.

However, from all that I know of the Iranians, I believe
that in time the fanaticism of the Revolution will pass. I
can think of no better support for this than the nature of
Iranian pilgrimage and the shrines which are its object.
Iranians are much prone to pilgrimage, for though they
love the flesh, they love the spirit too—perhaps not quite
the contradiction that some in the West might think. And
they certainly have much opportunity for pilgrimage since
Iran is covered with shrines, everything from little wayside
places to the great edifices in the holy cities—some of the
latter among the most dazzling buildings in the East. Not
one of these thousands of shrines honors a soldier or a
political figure. All are dedicated to either saints or poets.
In the end, these, rather than the bullhorns, are the voices
that the Iranians heed and venerate.

In the meantime what, it might be asked, will be the effects of the revolution on the kinds of country places and
country people described in this book? There is an old
tag in the East which says that the emperor's writ ends at
the village gate. So does the revolution's. By and large,
who rules will not make much difference to these people
and places — whether it be a shah, an ayatollah, a presi-
dent, or a commissar. What does, and will, make the difference slipped through the village gate some time
ago — a tandem of two simple, mundane things: the transistor radio and the motorbike. These, more than all the
edicts of parties, councils, and rulers, will transform the
countryside, not only of Iran but of all the Middle East,
transform it by ending that isolation which fosters and
protects the traditional life.

This brings me to my reasons for writing this book.
Isolation and the traditional life have by no means disappeared from the Iranian countryside, but they are on
their way. In many respects this will be for the best. On

the other hand, there are certain features of the traditional life of the Iranians that I believe good and that I have loved with all my heart. Watching these things pass, I suppose it seemed to me that the only way to keep them — for myself and perhaps for others — was to gather them together into a book of recollection such as this.

I hope it is a just recollection. A Westerner in Iran inevitably misunderstands the country to some degree; his past and present are too different from those of the Iranian. "A foreigner may live here a hundred years but he will never really understand us," an old Iranian once said to me. And by then I knew enough to know that he was right.

This leads me to make an apology to the Iranians, my kind hosts for many years. Surely in some of the things I say about them I shall be wide of the mark; I hope they will forgive me.

Postscript, 1988

It is now ten years since the onset of the Iranian Revolution and eight years since the initial publication of this book. At the time I had forgotten that an alternate meaning of the word "revolution" is the meaning of "return."

Long ago Kipling told us that the "twain" of East and West would never meet. He was both right and wrong. In fact, there has been a junction but it has taken the form of a collision rather than a meeting; a collision in which the Middle Easterner has been injured, left dazed, confused. And, of course, the natural reaction to collison is recoil.

To switch analogies, there is a saying in the Middle East that the stranger's cloak is never warm. And indeed the cloak of the West has proven chill and really does not fit. Why should it? After all, it was designed for another people, another climate. So the Iranians, among others, have thrown it off and gone back to the native garment they know best. Paradoxically, then, the descriptions of life found in this book are in many ways more apt today than for the time when they were written. It is verses from the Koran that the people now hear on their transistor radios rather than the latest jazz, and as for the motorbikes, these carry them not out into the world but rather to their shrines.

BESMELLAH, ARRAHMAN, ARRAHIM

In the name of God, the most merciful and compassionate.

Prologue

Garden of the Brave in War

I WENT TO IRAN IN 1957 — went out of curiosity, stayed out of interest and much affection. I lived first in the city of Isfahan in central Iran, teaching at its university and enjoying the place, for Isfahan is one of the most beautiful cities in the world. It had, however, been my experience in other countries where the traditional life is still lived that the heart of such places is in the countryside, not in the cities, where indeed the old life passes first. Also, I have always been fond of country life. So when I heard through a friend that a farm in the region of Fars, down toward the gulf, could be leased cheaply and that it appeared to suit my other needs as well, I did not hesitate to make the necessary arrangements to go there to live.

The place had a curious history. It was called *Baugh-a-Salar Jang* — "Garden of the Brave in War" — after an old nobleman who had lived there some years before my time. Iranian titles were descriptive: the man had been brave in war, so when ennobled by a shah he was called what he had been. *Baugh,* which for some reason is usually translated into English as "garden," means, in fact, an orchard, and that is what the farm in general was.

Salar Jang was an unusual man. At some point he was appointed tax collector of the province, but instead of settling in the town, the normal thing to do, he chose to live in the Garden, which was some distance from the town and an isolated place. It was a daring thing to do for there was the good possibility, as there would be even today, of attack by brigands or by the tribes, and so to defend himself he kept a small, private garrison. When I came to the Garden the stump of their watch tower was still standing.

Not only did Salar Jang live in the Garden but he also conducted his affairs from there. He set up the first telephone line in the province, running between the Garden and the tax office in the town. Also, there were those cellars beneath the salon of the house, the hasps and chains still in the walls when I arrived, for he had used the cellars as dungeons for delinquent taxpayers.

The cellars may suggest that Salar Jang was an extortionist rather than a proper tax collector, but from all that I had heard he was a just man and actually represented, in many ways, the old ideal of an Iranian gentleman. He was a good poet, an accomplishment as necessary in those days as knowing how to ride and shoot. Also, he was extravagantly hospitable. The old gardener, whom I inherited with the place, told me that in Salar Jang's time the guests were so common that they killed a dozen chickens a day. Further, he provided his guests with good entertainment. In that part of Iran today, as in the past, there are Jewish musicians, though minstrels might be the more accurate term, and it is common to hire them for an evening party or picnic. Salar Jang hired them, and the best of them, to play in the Garden by the season, that is, from mid-spring through early autumn. Finally, he was known everywhere for his love of the flesh, especially the flesh of fat women.

For how many years Salar Jang lived on in the Garden with his poetry, minstrels, fat women, and guests, I do not know; but at some point he was driven out. A tribe whose summer pastures were to the west of the farm attacked and occupied the place. He apparently had some warning — perhaps a lookout on the watchtower, scanning the desert through the telescope, saw the tribe riding down in force, too great a force for his little garrison to oppose. In any event, he managed to get away in time with his carpets, books, and silver braziers. Only a rosewood piano was left.

The tribe held the Garden for six weeks. The tribe's khan lived in the house; his men camped around in the orchards and farm buildings, and from the Garden they would make periodic attacks on the town. Finally, however, they were routed and Salar Jang was able to come back.

But the place had been devastated, all the stained glass lights of the greenhouse shot out in target practice, the trees completely stripped of fruit — and an Iranian values the fruit of a good season as much as a Frenchman values the wines of a good vintage. They said that the old man took sick in grief at what had happened to his Garden. In any event, not long after his return he died.

The place was inherited by two sons who, according to the local people, were "bad seed." They were without accomplishments, gross in their pleasures, and entirely improvident. One of the sons, the old gardener told me, "had no beard," and when women were brought to him — the gardener disdainfully waggled a limp finger. It was this son who one night stabbed to death a gardener's boy in a corner of the farmyard. And that, for a time, was the end of the Garden. The place got a bad name, the sons went elsewhere, and the ownership passed to a merchant in the town. The merchant made a few alterations in the house but rarely used it. When I went there to live the place had been deserted for over twenty years.

It was then more a jungle than a garden — the trees grappled together, the buildings weighed down with creepers, the doorways like the openings of caves in a tangled mountainside. Those first nights it was difficult to sleep through the screaming of the jackals who for so long had made the place their home. In time, however, we got it into shape — the orchards and the vineyards pruned, the creepers cut away, the high walls of hedges trimmed down to a proper height, new gravel in the walks. There was work to do on the buildings as well: paint and plaster, new beams, window glass, a stable to reroof. By the time we were finished, it had, I hope, some resemblance to the days when Salar Jang led his good life there.

The main house looked more like a fort than a house. It had mud-brick walls five feet thick, plastered and whitewashed over, and a pierced parapet around the roof. Standing there strong and square and white, guarding the oasis, it could well have had pennants flying from it. A flight of stone steps at the center of the main facade led up into an arch-windowed gallery which ran the length of the house. On the other side of this, through a barrel vault — it was, I believe, the key vault of the building — lay the salon, a big, high-ceilinged room with a fireplace in each corner and a floor of black and white parquet. There was little in the room — an armoire, some brass-plaqued Bombay chests, a sofa, and a few prim chairs — for we seldom used it, though once we held a dance there. The room I lived in was off to one side of the house; it was a combination study and office, a crammed and cluttered room with deep window embrasures and fine views.

In front of the house there was a clay-cobbled yard about the size of a tennis court, shaded by a half-dozen old plane trees. A long, horizontal pool lay along the far edge of the yard; beyond it stretched a hundred feet of meadow lawn bordered on either side by graveled walks and these in turn by hedges. At the end stood a platonic tree, a high, perfectly formed walnut, its branches like a fan against the sky. The alley began on the far side of the walnut; it was the finest alley in the countryside, almost a quarter of a mile of ancient cypress with a lush greensward between them. The orchards were to the left and right of these, the vineyards at the end. If one stood below the barrel arch of the salon, the whole vista lay spread out before one: the cobbled yard, the pool, the lawn, the walnut, and finally the marching cypress of the alley. Like a passage of perfect music, or a perfect passage in a book, it stilled one, and for the moment there was order and beauty.

Both the garden and the house had many felicities. In the English basements there were a summer sitting room and a bedroom: cool, white, green-shuttered rooms. The sitting room was equipped with a device peculiar to Iran, so far as I know, and called a *badgir,* a "wind catcher." This was a shaft at the back of the room that passed up through the house and into a high chimney louvered at the top. The chimney sucked down the "wind," and thus the sitting room was always ventilated by a current of cool, fresh air. And there was a tiled pool in the room so situated that the air current passed across the surface of the water, rippling it. Water, for Iranians, is a material to be worked with as much as steel and concrete are for people in other places.

In the garden, too, water had been put to graceful use. At the center of the north orchard we had something called a *bonigah.* This was a two-foot-high circular platform of clay cobbles surrounded by a two-foot-wide stone

7

channel of running water, which, in turn, was bordered by a circle of plane trees. Set around and on the platform were a dozen socketed granite blocks into which torches could be put. It was a place to go at night, lay carpets, light the torches, and then listen to the water and watch its flashings in the torch light.

There was also another place to go at night called the *mahtabi*. It was in no way connected with water, but it was connected with light — and Iranians are about as obsessed with light as they are with water; they love gems, pyrotechnic displays, mirrors, the reflecting surfaces of pools, the sun, and moonlight. On full moon nights we would hear the drums, from all over the oasis, of people who had come out from the village to picnic in the moonlight. Our *mahtabi*, which means "a place of moonlight," was a small, balustraded terrace on top of one of the outbuildings. It had been put in that particular place because no trees were close enough to screen the sky from view. On full moon nights it was a splendid place for making love.

Then, in winter, there was the study fire and, on rare evenings, the salon, lit by the old lopsided pewter chandeliers and by the corner fireplaces burning walnut logs.

Salar Jang had fitted out his Garden for repose. It is one of the purposes of a garden in Iran — a place to enjoy idleness and languor, to feel coolness and warmth, to gaze at greenness and water, to listen to bird song, poetry, and music — a refuge from the turmoil Iranians have so often known. The Old Persian word for a garden is *perdows,* the root word of our word *paradise.*

But an Iranian garden also serves another purpose, for the Iranians, eminently romantic, are also extremely pragmatic. In the West these are incongruities, but in Iran they are not. That decorative ring of water which surrounded the *bonigah* was there to irrigate the orchard. In other words, the Garden was also a farm and it was meant to make money.

The biggest crop on our roughly thirty acres was pomegranates. This, perhaps, was the reason that the main motif in the plaster work of the salon fireplaces and in the cornices of the rooms was a pomegranate. We harvested the pomegranates in the fall and stored them in big heaps in the farmyard through the winter, selling them off when the prices were good. Our second crop was grapes, small, tightly clustered purple grapes from which the winery in the town made a pungent, heavy brandy. In good years we sold walnuts, too, but more often we bartered off our small surplus of walnuts for limes brought in from the gulf to juice for winter use. The other fruits of the place — apples, pears, plums, and quinces — we kept for ourselves or gave away. We had only one other money crop and a queer one it was — dog roses. From the ten big dog rose bushes, each with a circumference of about twenty feet, we stripped the blossoms and distilled them to make a liquor which we sold to the villagers. They in turn made it into a kind of elixir.

We kept livestock too. We had some sheep, selling off the lambs to the village butchers, buying sometimes from the shepherds who drove their flocks by the farm in the spring on their way to the high country. Then there were chickens, a big bell cage of partridge, three dogs, an Arab mare, and even, for a time, an ill-tempered monkey pawned off on us by some gypsies who turned up one year selling baskets.

. Finally, there were all the odds and ends of work: a kitchen garden, bees, always wood to saw and chop, the awful job of cleaning out the reservoir, a greenhouse to tend, the pots of geraniums — dozens of them scattered under the plane trees — to be watered all through the spring and summer and to take cuttings from each fall. We spent much time, too, getting ready for the winter. There were the limes, pomegranates, and sour cherries to juice; melons, potatoes, and fruit to put down in straw; all kinds of preserves and pickles to be made; and eternally that wood to saw and chop.

All in all, there was enough to keep us busy, though not so much that we were driven, not that. The profits were modest but still sufficient to keep in a good supply of vodka, to send for books, to buy gas for the Landrover, to pay the servants, to take a journey now and then; in short, enough to live there in a simple and, on the whole, quite satisfactory way. More, I suppose, could have been made, but the extra time seemed more important than the extra profits. After all, there were the *bonigah*, the *mahtabi*, the cypress alley, the study fire, and also the countryside around the farm to walk and ride in.

The farm was in an oasis, the oasis in a desert, and the desert was a plain between two ranges of mountains. The oasis itself consisted of about three square miles of orchards, vineyards, the occasional alley of cypress, and a few fine coppices of poplar. The orchards and vineyards belonged mainly to the peasants in the village, who walked out or rode donkey-back to tend them.

The oasis owed its existence to a *qanat*. A *qanat* is a manmade underground channel that brings water from a mountain spring down into a plain. Ours began ten miles away on the lower slopes of the north mountain range, surfacing again near the farm at a place called the *maqsam*, a pool about an acre in extent. Over forty open channels fanned out from this pool through the oasis, watering it. If the spring had dried up or the *qanat* caved in, the oasis might well have disappeared, gone back to desert.

Except for the vineyards and orchards, there was not

much of note in our oasis. A few clay lanes wound through, bordered by high clay walls with a peak of thatching along their tops. In summer these lanes were ravines of baked clay and dust. Yet in the early morning or evening they were pleasant places to walk or ride in. At almost any point, one could hear the sound of running water in the gardens beyond the walls, and above the walls themselves there was usually a green frieze of trees. In winter, though, after rains, the lanes were quagmires, and when snow came, impassable. We were rather high there, more than four thousand feet above the gulf.

We had, too, a few sights in our oasis, though perhaps it's dignifying them too much to call them that. One was a mill, a low, clay building with a squat tower, set at a crossroads, an old walnut in front of it under which the miller used to sit on summer afternoons smoking his water pipe.

Another of our sights was a holy tree, a plane some eighty feet high which stood in a clearing watered by a tiny spring. The local people believed that a holy man had once stopped there and that God, to commemorate his visit, had willed this tree to grow — how else to account for a tree so old and gigantic? It was a place of pilgrimage for the villagers, its lower limbs always fluttering with bits of colored votive cloth, and usually a few candles burned in the brass-grilled cavity set into its trunk.

Finally, there was "the statue of the king." Actually, the statue was a life-sized bas-relief cut into an outcrop of rock that rose in the center of one of the poplar coppices. Here, too, there was a tiny spring. The bas-relief, most people thought, was of Shapur I, who ruled Iran in the third century. Perhaps because of time, perhaps because it was never finished, the figure of the little king there in the ocher-colored rock was rather dim, but one could still make out the drape lines of his cloak, the curls flowing out from under the flared crown, the raised, benedictive hand. No one knew why the king was there. Perhaps he had won a battle at that spot or had a son born to him, or perhaps he had come that way before the time of the *qanat* and oasis, and his men, in gratitude for his leading them to water, had carved out this remembrance of him.

Such, then, was the oasis. Except for summer midday and during the rains and snows of winter, it was, as I have said, a pleasant place to walk and ride. There was also good shooting: snipe at the *maqsam* at dusk and partridge almost everywhere in the early morning.

Beyond the oasis, on all sides, lay the desert. For a brief time at dawn and dusk, it was the most soothing landscape in the world, spreading out in utter peace. The rest of the day, at least in summer, it was an unspeakable inferno. The sand was mixed with mica which flashed cruelly in the sun, cutting the eyes and throat like little knives; and in the terrible blast of its dryness, the body, and for that matter the mind, shriveled like paper in a flame.

Finally, there were the mountains. They rose up two thousand feet on either side of us, ending the desert, putting a limit to the sky, enclosing and protecting us, and giving us the feeling that we inhabited a special, defined place on the surface of the earth, not just some speck in the midst of vastness.

They were grim guardians — massive, barren, no roundness or swell to them, no softness. Their colors, though, were magnificent; at midday they lay there tawny as lions in the sun, while at dusk they glowed like banked coals, slowly paling down to salmon, then to plum, and finally to the deep blue of the night sky itself. Only on those rare days when we had no sun did they go sullen, grey as lead. No one lived in them, but there were mountain rams, wild boars, wolves, gazelles and leopards. I like to hunt, but I seldom went to the mountains. I felt somehow that I had no business there.

There was another reason, as well, why the presence of the mountains meant much to us. They were our yang. The oasis was almost too voluptuous, too languorous with all its water, leaf, and blossom. The mountains, on the other hand, were naked, hard, and lasting — the bone to our flesh.

That, then, was the Garden and its immediate environs. I lived there alone except for a house servant named Mamdali and his wife and children, plus the old gardener, Ra'is Ali, and his "assistants," two little boys of eight and ten. At harvest time we brought in extra men to help, and in the early spring, some itinerant laborers would come for a few weeks and stay with us to spade the orchards and the vineyards.

Like all old places, the Garden was haunted — haunted, I suppose, by the spirits of the old libertine, Salar Jang, and the murdered gardener's boy. Indeed we often knew sheer joy at the Garden, but sometimes, too, tragedy whipped down on us, suddenly out of nowhere, like the "poisoned wind" which on occasion blew in from the desert and turned the leaves of the orchard black. More usual though were the long, still days when little seemed to happen except the movement of the sun along its arc. The Garden was like a life.

The Keeper of the Garden

Not long after coming to the farm, I realized that Ra'is Ali, the old gardener I had inherited with the place, was incapable of carrying out the duties of a house servant. He could prepare a good omelet but that was all, and I grew tired of omelets. As for the house, he made only token efforts to keep down the cobwebs and dust. There was no alternative but to get another servant.

It happened that I mentioned the matter to a shoemaker I knew in town. He was a man I admired much for being both carefree and devout, and so when he suggested that a cousin of his might work out for me, I was interested; in Iran, when one takes a wife or a servant, the character of the sponsor is of much importance. Also, the cousin, like the shoemaker, was from one of the villages of Yezd, an isolated desert town in the east whose inhabitants had kept many of the old virtues. Accordingly, it was arranged that the cousin should come to me for a trial period of a month. His name was Mohammed Ali but he was called Mamdali for short.

I have not forgotten my first sight of Mamdali, for he was somewhat more the country cousin than I had expected. He wore white cloth slippers with soles of camel bone, baggy black trousers, a shawl round his waist, and a long kind of Chinese coat — a costume which, since a former shah decreed the wearing of Western dress, one rarely sees anymore except in the most remote of places. What he brought with him, wrapped in a checkered cloth, bespoke a deep country background: some pomegranates, two cloth bags of nuts, the Koran, a prayer stone, wool and knitting needles, spare pajamas and shirts, a little mirror and a pair of clippers — the last indicating that like his cousin, the shoemaker, he was a stickler for the religious law and clipped his beard instead of shaving it.

Mamdali was then in his middle twenties, squat, bow-legged, and rather Tibetan in his features — and indeed he probably had some Mongol soldier ancestor, coming as he did from the east of Iran. But the thing that struck me, and for that matter anyone who ever saw him, was his smile. It was the smile of someone who has just arrived in the world and finds it a delight. For me, however, that first time, it was a frightening smile, expressing, so it seemed, such a vast innocence, such unbounded trust. I wanted to yell out to him, "Be careful! Watch out! Run! Hide!" I was mistaken in this judgement, as things turned out: he was entirely capable of taking care of himself — and of me as well.

That smile of innocence and the extraordinary competence were gradually reconciled for me as I realized that he had a simple, folk mind with a very quick intelligence. It was an interesting combination, though at first — and to some extent always — a most puzzling one. Here was a man who could solve an everyday problem better than almost anyone I had ever known but who, at the same time, believed that the world rested on the horns of an enormous ox. Perhaps to some people this would not come as a shock, but to me it did, and again and again I was taken aback by the antipodes of his mind. Slowly, however, and as I learned more about his background, both from himself and from visits to his village, the contradictions began to blur; I ceased, almost, to split him down the middle with my notions, and began to take him for the very whole man he was.

The village he came from was a classic desert one. It

looked as if the earth had heaved up into mounds, only the rims of things making a break with the desert, the green all hidden behind clay walls. At the center there was a small *maidan,* a square, a mosque at one end of it, a caravanserai at the other, while along the sides were shops selling simple things like sugar, tea, and matches. From the *maidan* narrow lanes snaked out into a ring of dwellings, a dense, toppling, hodgepodge of earthen walls and domes with here and there a bath, a shrine, a domed reservoir. The house Mamdali's mother lived in was like most of the houses in the place. It had a barrel vault of baked mud open to a courtyard, a small room adjoining each side of the vault. Bedding, carpets, and some cooking pots furnished it.

Each year when the mulberries came on, his mother would leave this house and go to a walled orchard she owned on the outskirts of the village. Here she lived through the summer in a little hut, weaving and tending her trees, staying on until autumn and the harvests of the last fruits. Then with winter she would return to her house in the village.

Most of the villagers migrated for the summer to the nearby fields and orchards, where they appeared to provide themselves with almost everything they needed: sheep, vegetables, fruit, and wheat. They had little contact with the outside except for the passing caravans, and they brought nothing new. The old life was still lived there.

As far as I could gather from my visits to the village and from Mamdali himself, this life consisted of three things: God, nature, and other people.

God's law, which is to say the law of Islam, covered almost everything. There may have been people there who observed the Iranian civil calendar, but I doubt that there

were many — Mamdali certainly did not. For most people, the year was marked off by the birth and death days
of the Imams, the early leaders of Shiah Islam; by the
seasons of fasting, mourning, and pilgrimage; and by
those other deeply religious occasions — birth, marriage,
and death. No act was commenced without asking God's
grace — his compassion and mercy — nor concluded without praising his bounty.

Then there was their attitude toward nature. It was not
so much that they lived close to it as in it. The weather,
animals, soil, and crops — they mingled with these things,
caring for them, fighting them, and in the end taking
them, directly and without intermediary, to themselves — the wool, meat, fruit, and grains, the shade of
trees, charcoal's warmth. They did not think of people,
animals, and trees as belonging to different orders. How
could they, when so patently all followed the same course,
began from root, grew, blossomed, made seed, bore fruit,
decayed?

Finally, there was the relationship of the people to each
other. It was, it seemed to me, a symbiotic one, an
ecology of people. It took the form of a fraternity,
though not a fraternity of equals. There were older
brothers and younger brothers, the wise and the stupid,
the powerful and the weak, the good, the bad — still,
nonetheless, all brothers. From things I heard, there
were, I believe, some Cains in that fraternity, but that did
not negate the fact that the people lived, and to a degree
which I had rarely seen before, with responsibility for one
another.

I mention these things about the village — the closeness
of God, of nature, and of people to each other — because
Mamdali brought these things to the farm along with his
looking glass and his bags of nuts. They were strange

and not always comfortable presences to live with. In the beginning, for example, it deeply irritated me that whenever I stated an intention, he would add for me, since I had neglected it, "God willing." I did not care to be crossed in my belief that my acts were willed by me.

I was often brought up short by the very different ways in which we regarded the natural world. For me nature was a system of impersonal forces which by some accident had come into being. For him these forces were the wishes of God and, in addition, had personality. One day, not thinking particularly of what I was saying, I asked him why we always had such heavy winds in late winter. "God has sent them to wake the trees," he said, and he pointed out the window at the moving branches. "Yes," he went on, "now they wake and the sap will begin to run. And of course," he winked, "the winds come to wake and play with us as well."

But the most baffling thing of all was Mamdali's concept of our relationship as master and servant. As far as I was concerned, at least in the beginning, his role as a servant was to cook, wash dishes, and scrub the floor, while my duty as a master was to pay his salary once a month. He saw things quite differently. What was important was my well-being, physical and spiritual, not my floors and dishes, of which, in fact, he took little notice. As for the role of master, Mamdali soon made it clear that payment of the monthly salary was the least of it.

On the afternoon of his arrival, I sat down with Mamdali to work out a written program of his duties, complete with headings and subheadings, and I asked him to commit it to memory. It did not take long for this program to disappear and be replaced by what I think might be termed his rhythm, a rhythm that varied according to mood, weather, the events of the day, and, most importantly, "God's will." There were, however, some constants.

His first act of the day was to get up on the roof of his house and pray. Next he would enter my bedroom and in a loud voice announce, "Wake and wash yourself." This would be followed, after an interval, by a knock on the dressing room door and the question, "Are you an Arab or an Iranian?" If I was naked, I would answer that I was an Arab and he would wait outside the door, whereas if I was clothed, or partly so, I would reply that I was an Iranian and he would come in with the coffee. This, of course, was a joke reflecting the old Iranian view that Arabs were uncivilized people who went about unclothed and ate lizards.

While I shaved and drank the coffee, we would ask each other about our respective night's rests and then proceed to an examination of any dreams we might have had. I could bring to bear only the crudest of Freudian interpretations, but Mamdali worked from a highly detailed system in which every color, movement, and form had its meaning. After advising me, on the basis of my dreams, about what occasions and persons I should avoid, or vice versa, through the day, he would serve breakfast.

Having aired the kitchen of the noxious odors of the "forbidden meat of pig," i.e., my bacon, and doing a rather slapdash job on the dishes, Mamdali would leave the house, and I would not see much of him again unless I rang. Outside he occupied himself in various ways, the most common being the repairing and making of things. There was much of the former to do, as there is on any farm. He could plaster, put in glass, carpenter, do wir-

ing, and make simple repairs on the old Landrover and
the pump, both of which broke down often. All these
tasks he approached with the greatest common sense. I
once gave him a cooking pot which had a small hole in its
side and told him to take it to the tinner. Instead, he put
a match in the hole and we used the pot for the rest of
our time at the farm.

He also thoroughly enjoyed making things: fine baskets
from the willow branches; rope from accumulated string;
toys for his children — slingshots, whistles, kites, whirl-
igigs; a weather vane; a tree house; birdcages; a leather
cradle for his baby.

The activity that occupied most of his time in this cate-
gory was knitting. In his village the women wove, the
men knitted, and so Mamdali provided not only his family
but also me with all the sweaters, caps, scarves, socks, and
mittens we needed. When there was no other chore to
do, he would sit cross-legged in a chair by the fire, or in
warm weather on the cobbles by the pool, and knit — the
yarn threaded and held out from himself by his big toe —
improvising with colors and patterns as he went along.
Once he made me a pair of mittens from undyed wool.
"They are very plain," he said on finishing them, and so
"to make them pretty," he embroidered a red flower on
the back of each. Once, too, he held up a sweater he had
started and said, "I think I shall put a man in it," and
then, with a raised stitch which an Aran Islander might
have envied, he filled the front panel of the sweater with a
saluting warrior. When the sweater was finished, I found
he had knitted in "the man's horse," on the back of it.

Another important part of Mamdali's daily rhythm consisted of calls he made on his family. Repairing to his
quarters adjoining the greenhouse as a sultan repairs to
his harem, he would sprawl against big bolsters, playing

THE KEEPER OF THE GARDEN

with his children, teaching them *ta'arof* — the complicated
forms of Iranian etiquette — and being fed and enter-
tained by his wife. Khanom — translated into English it
can mean "Madam," and I always addressed her as that —
Khanom was an excellent mimic. In the warm months
when the windows were open, I would hear them all in
convulsions of laughter. Khanom was doing one of her
imitations, sometimes, no doubt, of me.

On principle I did not interfere in their lives, nor did I
enter their quarters except on the eve of the Iranian New
Year, when they would entertain me for dinner. Nonetheless, I could not help being aware of some of their living habits. One of the most singular was that they did not
eat according to any schedule. Mamdali might take his
lunch at eleven in the morning, or take no lunch at all; his
son, Nasair, might eat at four, Khanom at noon, his daughter, Batul, at yet another time. No one ate until he or she
was hungry.

Another curious but pleasing little habit they had was
that of the night teas. One of the children, or Mamdali,
or Khanom, might wake in the night and want company,
and so would wake the others — like many Iranians, they
slept all together in one big nest of comforters. They
would make tea, chat a little, and then go back to sleep.
Sometimes, too, in winter, just before the dawn, they
would go outside, build a fire, and boil some turnips. Occasionally I would rise early to go shooting and would see
them there, the dogs as well, squatting by the fire in the
frost and vapors of the early morning, and they would call
me to join them. According to Mamdali, eating hot,
salted turnips on a winter morning was, like love, one of
the great pleasures of life.

That, then, was Mamdali's usual day: preparing my
meals, flipping now and then at the cobwebs and the dust,

for the most part, though, tinkering at something outside, stopping when he felt like it to call on his family. He had, too, his night work — no part of my original program for him — which consisted of his rounds, a walk around the boundaries of the farm once before he went to bed and once again between midnight and dawn. Because we lived in an isolated place, he was convinced that "the thieves" would come unless proper precautions were taken. In addition to the rounds, these precautions included keeping the dogs chained in a dark place for part of the day so that they would roam at night, and purchasing a parrot which he tried, without success, to teach to say "thief" on seeing a stranger.

Mamdali took no day off, though the original program had called for one. Apparently he did not feel the need. "A day off from what?" I think he would have asked.

As I mentioned earlier, Mamdali brought to the farm three things which were strange to me: his concept of the natural world, his belief that God lives down among us, and his idea of how people should live together. His natural world contained many more wonders than my own and was a far more interesting, if peculiar, place.

One day a jet passed over the Garden. I, rather pompously, began to explain why the sound of the jet did not reach us until the jet had passed. This, he said, was interesting, but did I know how the sky had gotten up there in the first place. "Up there?" I asked, perplexed. Then he proceeded to tell me the explanation he had heard from an old man, emphasizing the oldness of the man several times before beginning — for this, after all, bore on the validity of the theory. In the past, he said, the sky, like the tree branches, was close to the earth. Then it happened one day that an old woman was up on the roof washing diapers. When she finished, she put her hand up to wipe it on the sky. The sky then rose and since that day has been far above us.

He must have noted the incredulous look on my face, for he repeated that the man who had told the story had been very old. It reminded me of the evening when he was lighting the fire with an old copy of *Time* magazine and I happened to explain to him *Time*'s practice of choosing the most important man of the year for its New Year cover. "Oh, I see," he said. "You mean the oldest man in your country." And there came on his face that smile, musing and tender, which always appeared when to him the world seemed right.

Then there was the case of Fatima Khanom, "Miss Fatima," a small variety of owl which lived in the trees of the cobbled yard. Mamdali took a special, angry interest in Fatima Khanom. One spring he removed six baby bluebirds from their nest and put them in a cage, caring for them with much devotion, for he was very fond of birds. Not long after, Fatima Khanom, forcing her head through the bars of the cage, killed all six of them. "Next spring," Mamdali said, "I shall find Fatima's nest and kill every one of her babies." And he did just that, thoroughly enjoying his revenge.

One summer evening we were sitting out under the trees, entertaining a Tehran cousin of Mamdali's who had come for a visit, when it happened that Fatima Khanom flew overhead.

"There she goes, that Fatima Khanom," said Mamdali, glancing up with an angry, glint-eyed look.

"Mamdali!" the cousin said reprovingly. "What are you saying? In all the best zoos of Iran that bird is called an owl. Fatima Khanom indeed!"

"I do not know what she is called in the zoos or in your

books, but as far as I know she is Fatima Khanom." Then he turned to me. "There was once a child called Fatima who repeatedly disobeyed her mother. The mother told her to 'fly away,' which she did, and, well —" he motioned toward the tree branches, "that is Fatima Khanom — and still a mischief-maker."

"Mamdali," said the cousin, who was a high-school graduate, "only people who are uneducated believe such things."

"Humph," replied Mamdali. And then he looked up at the stars and began to hum, the sign that he declined to argue.

And so it went, everything in nature having its story — the world, his world at any rate, the richer for it. All things, too, had their purpose: the winds which wake the trees, the dewlaps which "ornament" a goat, the sun which leaves the day sky to rest for the night, even bats.

"I detest bats," I once said.

"Oh, you mustn't do that," Mamdali replied.

"And why not?"

"Don't you know that the bats break the webs woven by the spiders and that without the bats we would wake in the morning to find the world enclosed in a cocoon?"

Only in one respect was his cosmology incomplete. He had never seen the sea and had no real idea of its nature. This bothered him, and he would often ask me questions about it. Would I imitate its sound? How deep and long was it? Why should it be blue? But I don't think he ever really comprehended, despite all my explanations, for one night he said to me, "And are there camels in the sea?"

Concerning God, however, there were no uncertainties. Not long after Mamdali's arrival, the farm became a small theocracy with him as its governing priest. The day began and ended with prayer. All holidays, sad as well as joyous, were strictly observed. During Ramazan, the month of fasting, I saw little of him in the day, for he would sleep in order to circumvent the pangs of his hunger and thirst. In Moharram and Safar, the months of mourning, he wore black from head to toe, and there was little levity: no banging on a tambourine, none of the usual salacious jokes, the radio not only turned off but unplugged from its socket. There was also the yearly pilgrimage to the holy city of Meshed. Into the checkered cloth he would put a change of clothing, some simple provisions, the chains for flagellation, a bottle of rose water with which to perfume the other pilgrims, and then set off, returning three weeks later, grave and bearded and with a certain holier-than-thouness which took some days to dissipate.

These observances did not affect my own life to any degree, but there were two aspects of his zeal that did extend to me and of which I often ran afoul. These were his concepts of sin and grace.

Many, many things were sinful and often, at least to my sense, unexpectedly so. Once a friend gave me some partridge. I am fond of partridge, and since there were few to be found for shooting in that season, I ordered Mamdali to kabob one for my dinner. "It has sin," he replied. And why, I asked. Because the partridge were beautiful and it would be sinful to kill such beauty. A few days later, however, something happened which I thought would assure me of a partridge dinner. One of the birds was found dead in the room in which we were temporarily keeping them — had flown against the window, I assumed. This, then, I would eat. But no. That, too, had sin, for in Islam no animal that has died of an unknown cause may be eaten. Time passed and with it, I assumed, Mamdali's appreciation of the partridges' beauty, and so once more I suggested partridge for dinner. But yet again I ran afoul of sin, for it was the mating season, and in this season — and during the time that animals nurse their young — it is forbidden to kill them. I gave up.

Another instance of sinfulness was my practice of bathing naked in the pool. Mamdali, I knew, disapproved, for according to religious law exposure of the genitals is decidedly sinful. But here I put my foot down. After all, when I was bathing he and his family could keep their distance. Nonetheless, I knew that he was not happy about this transgression, and so one day I gave him a brief lecture, pointing out that God had given us our member and thus it could not be considered bad. "It is not bad," he replied. "But if God had wanted it displayed, he would have put it on your neck." He strode off, calling back, "It has sin."

Then there were those actions that please God and earn us his grace. I could hardly be expected to go on pilgrimage, to fast, to say the daily prayers, but still there were a large number of actions which Mamdali believed it behooved me to perform. He often urged me to be more generous in giving alms. If I fell out with someone, he was quick to insist on *ashti*, the special Islamic ritual of forgiveness and reconciliation. If I was tardy in visiting a sick friend, or if there was too long a delay in answering the letters of persons with requests or in misfortune, he brought it to my attention. A good friend died during my time at the farm. Mamdali would not let me forget that an occasional visit to his grave was in order. Finally, there was our yearly *nazr*. Once, when I was driving in the mountains, the steering on the Landrover went out about a hundred yards before a stretch of road that bordered a precipice. If the failure had occurred a few moments later, it would have been the end of us. In thanks for God's protection, Mamdali recommended that we prepare a *nazr* — that is, kill a sheep and make a feast for the poor of our neighborhood — and further that we repeat this *nazr* on each anniversary of the accident. And so we did.

All of this may suggest that Mamdali was a pious old stick. That was not at all the case. He had a very bawdy tongue and thoroughly enjoyed the pleasures of the flesh. On Thursday night, more or less the official night for lovemaking in Iran, I was lucky if I got my dinner, so frankly anxious was he to get off to bed. And he loved to play practical jokes. Cigarettes exploded, and plastic scorpions and other insects were forever appearing in my bed and at the bottom of my coffee cup.

Another of his jokes, of which fortunately I was not a victim, was something called "cork tea." He once gave it to a man from the village who used to bore us by calling on us too frequently. Cork tea was made by boiling a cork in water. This beverage, according to Mamdali, produced such extreme flatulence that "the fellow will have to ring a bell in front of himself for three days in order to disguise his explosions."

The best of his jokes stemmed from a gift my sister once sent me, a small, bronze Buddha. Not knowing the Iranian word for statuette, and wanting also to tease him for being superstitious, I told him that the Buddha was a jinni. The next morning he told me that neither he nor his wife had been able to sleep due to various annoyances caused by the jinni. I laughed and told him that I had only been teasing him. Nonetheless, the complaints continued. Finally, fed up, I gave him a lecture on superstition and told him not to bother me with the matter again. That afternoon I went as usual to the summer bedroom to take a nap. I had hardly fallen asleep when I was awakened by peculiar noises and the shaking of the bed. There was no one in the room, nor was the room itself shaking, though we sometimes had slight earthquakes. For a moment half my mind, perhaps three-fourths, considered the jinni. Then I heard the giggling, and Mamdali and Khanom crawled out from under the bed.

So there was much playfulness in his nature, or at any rate on the surface of it. For this lightness, though a part of his everyday life, lay on him as lines of ornament lie on damask steel. Below was a stern conscientiousness. I have already mentioned how this conscientiousness concerned itself with my spiritual well-being. My physical state, too, was carefully regarded.

Mamdali and his wife, like most villagers, were versed in herbal medicines, and I was often dosed with these. Sometimes the doses were administered without my asking for them. Mamdali would note some symptom — paleness, a cough, poor appetite — and I would find a dose set out on my desk, most commonly flower of cow's tongue tea.

Also, like most Iranians, he adhered to a caloric theory of foods which possibly came to Iran from the Greeks. Every food, according to this theory, is either "hot" or "cold," and hot and cold foods may be eaten only in certain combinations. In addition, many illnesses require a diet of either one or the other. Mamdali, insofar as was possible, attempted to impose this system on my eating habits. I often strayed, with the result that any indispositions brought forth a testy attitude of "I told you so."

Mamdali also had a habit of checking on me if I did not come home at night. Once it happened that I got into a street fight in the town and was badly injured. He had to nurse me for the week that I was in the hospital — a customary practice in Iran, rather than the patient hiring a nurse. This incident upset him, so that always after that when he did not find me at the farm in the morning, he would go to the town and inquire after me of everyone I knew. This meant, of course, that my philanderings became common knowledge. He was aware of this, but in his judgement, finding out what had happened to me was worth a little scandal.

My "face," too, was a subject of concern to him. For any people, face and not losing it are important, but this is particularly true of Iranians, far more so than of us. My battered old Landrover did not in my judgement reflect on me, but in his it did, and for that matter it reflected on him as my servant — and so I was always being urged to buy a "cadeelack."

An incident of this concern for face happened one Christmas when my sister and her husband came to spend the holidays with me. Mamdali had decided that his Christmas present to my sister would be a brass vial for kohl. But when it came time for him to wrap the present, I found that he had bought three vials, all identical. "But why three?" I asked. "To give only one would be ungenerous," he replied, and I knew that he believed that if he gave only one, I would lose face by being thought to have a skinflint as a servant.

On two occasions this face-saving had serious consequences, at least for the other people involved. One summer I went to spend a month on the Caspian coast. It happened that I knew an Iranian girl in Abadan who I thought would enjoy staying at the farm while I was gone. She was agreeable and came.

I had been at the Caspian for about two weeks when I woke one morning to find Mamdali kneeling at my bedside. Something clearly was wrong. No one makes a bus journey of nearly a thousand miles for nothing. Also, the kneeling suggested that he had done something which he was not altogether sure would meet with my approval.

The story came out. The people of the neighborhood and in the village had concluded that the girl was my fiancée — after all, she was living in my house. The fact that she was not my fiancée was of no importance compared with the fact of their belief. The girl, it seemed, had a male friend in the town, and he on several occasions had called on her. This was bad enough in Mamdali's judgement, but one night he saw them sitting side by side, "their knees touching!" Both were immediately driven from the farm, "and I banged the gate behind them," he added, eyes blazing. He did not say so, but the reason for his action was clear: he feared the local people would think that I was being cuckolded.

I should have learned my lesson from this incident but I did not. Some time later, intending to go to Europe for several months, I invited an American archaeologist and his wife to stay at the farm in my absence. It was not long before they too were driven out. Their sin, a most terrible one in Mamdali's judgement, was that of inhospitality: they did not offer guests refreshments, though he had urged them to do so. "Do they not know," said the letter which reached me in Paris, "that the guest is God, not some dog? I have put them out, for they were bringing disgrace on this place and yourself."

So Mamdali could go far in carrying out what he considered to be his duty toward me. The difference between him and a modern Western man in this respect was that his duty did not stop at that circle we draw around our independence, into which we believe no one has the right to step. He stepped right in, though not indiscreetly, if he sensed that there was trouble.

There was, for example, my habit — especially during the last years at the farm — of drinking rather heavily at night. He disapproved of this but put up with it, for after all I was not at fault for having been born into a benighted religion that permits intoxicants. Excess, however, he would not countenance. One of the first things he did each morning was fill the vodka decanter. If he found the decanter quite empty, he would take it to the dressing room and, standing in the doorway, hold it up for me to see, giving it a little shake to emphasize its emptiness.

One night I got so noisy in my drinking that he came in to see what was the matter. Finding that I was very drunk, he went to the sideboard and picked up the decanter. I told him to put it down, but he ignored me and started toward the kitchen. I went up to him and cursed him and told him to remember that he was my servant. He looked carefully at me, a worried expression appearing on his face, not because of what had happened — violent disputes between an Iranian servant and master are neither uncommon nor serious — but, as I realized later, because he had seen blood on my forehead from a fall I had taken earlier. Again I roared at him to leave the room, and he did, but only to return in a moment with a rope with which he tied me up and pulled me down the hall and put me on my bed. He left again, coming back with one of Khanom's doses — some mixture of opium and herbs — and asked me to drink it. I refused, so he engaged my arm in a hammer lock and I drank it.

I woke at dawn to find that the rope had been loosened. Looking around, I saw that he was still there, sitting on the floor against the wall, and from the way his head was tilted back I thought he was sleeping. But as the light grew stronger, I realized that his eyes were open, though heavy lidded, and that he was watching me — Mamdali, the keeper of the Garden, and of myself.

Journal I

SINCE THE WEATHER is warming up, I now spend more time in the garden and sometimes chat with Ra'is Ali, the gardener. He is a small, spare man with a skull of a head, flat, close-cut black hair, and little black eyes with lights. He moves — usually barefoot — with a kind of lope, but he can be very quick, a sudden scramble. He tells me that he is my slave and he does little things to ingratiate himself: picks flowers for me, brings fruit, showers me with compliments.

The other day he told me the story of a thief who once came to the Garden. There was, it seems, a raging wind — the time thieves strike, hoping that any noise they make will be mistaken for the creaks and bangings of a windy night. For this reason Ra'is Ali was particularly alert and, indeed, while making his rounds at midnight he came on a thief climbing to the roof of the house by means of a long stick. Ra'is Ali gave the stick a shake and the thief came sliding down. He then began to administer a beating, but the thief begged for mercy, promising not to come again. Ra'is Ali agreed to this, but before letting the thief go, he asked him how he had gotten into the garden. "I came," said the thief. This was not good enough. Finally the thief admitted to having come through a hole in the wall. "But I myself," said Ra'is Ali, "put a stone in that hole." "Yes," replied the thief, "but you did not plaster it in and the stone is loose."

Several weeks later, again on his rounds, who should Ra'is Ali come across but the same thief and this time halfway through the hole in the wall. "Now you will get

your beating," said Ra'is Ali. "But it is all your fault,"
cried the thief, "for you still have not plastered the stone
in."

Not long after, the thief died. This, according to Ra'is
Ali, was a pity, for the thief was "a clever man and stole
only bread."

The hives are full, so today we brought in a man from
the village to take the honey. When I went out to him in
the yard, he received me with the dignity and condescen-
sion of a great specialist. He is a tall, gangly fellow, perhaps once handsome, now worn out with drink and late
nights. On our way to the hives, he stopped at the greenhouse and, using one of the panes as a mirror, carefully
combed his greasy, thinning hair into a little curl above
each ear. Then he hung a cigarette on his lip and cocked
his head at himself, frowning. Finally, he turned to me
and said, "I am ready; please show me to the hives."

Hives here are shaped like kegs and made of clay. The
bee man said, "Besmellah, Arrahman, Arrahim" ("O God,
the most merciful and compassionate") — the formula
with which any work of moment is begun — and then
broke in the clay plug at the back of the hive. Next he
sheathed a stick in gunny and set it on fire. When the fire
had gone out, the gunny smoking, he poked the stick into
the hive to drive the bees to the rear and away from himself. "My saw, please," he said to Ra'is Ali, his assistant in
these operations — and a most nervous assistant he was,
leaping about with his coat over his head whenever a bee
zoomed out. Once he went off altogether, thrashing
through the trees. "Have you no courage?" the bee man
had bellowed at him.

With the saw, the bee man slowly cut away the comb from the walls of the hive, blowing cigarette smoke at the few bees that hopped and flew about. Laying the combs out on a brass tray, he brushed them with a fist of clover. "It is ripe and rich," he said. "Let us thank God for his bounty," said Ra'is Ali, and they did.

It was next my turn to give bounty — the bee man's fee. He asked for a figure which was outrageous. "No," I said, "I am tired of paying twice as much for everything simply because I am a foreigner." And I gave him a smaller wage. Believing, I suppose, that we must part with good feeling, he looked at the money and said, "Really I am not worthy even of this." Then he left, though stopping at the greenhouse once again to comb up the curls above his ears.

Yesterday I stopped at the Marnoon bridge to take some tea at the gendarme post and to watch the river. It is a pleasant spot. The bridge, small, old, and very solid, humps across the river with perfect grace, and there are poplars at either end of it. How well and agreeably they built bridges — not simply as a means to get to the other side but as places to stop and loiter and look down at the water.

Three girls were wading in the river. They were well covered by their chadors, their veils, except for their legs, which were bare to the knees and gleaming with water. Some gendarmes were watching them, rifles across their laps, their big, loose bodies sprawled on the river bank. One of them, his eyes narrowed against the smoke that curled up from his cigarette, had his hand between his legs, stroking himself. "Good ass," he said aloud but to himself.

At the time, a case was taking place at the gendarmerie. A young man with a loose but stubborn face sulked in one corner of the compound, while in another corner a girl crouched with an infant in her arms. Against a wall sat an old peasant smoking his pipe — the girl's father, I learned.

One of the gendarmes explained the situation to me. The girl had been the young man's maid and she claimed that the infant was his. Now she was at the gendarme post — the law in our parts — to have the matter settled by marriage or some money.

Not much appeared to be happening. The "law," a gendarme sergeant, walked casually around the compound as though taking a turn in his garden. Now and then he would stop to question the boy — who was sulky, sheepish, denying everything — and then, after a few more turns, he would speak with the girl. She said very little. She had no need to. There was the infant and there was her father, both in this situation weighing heavily.

Again the sergeant went back to taking his turns, head down, chin in his hands, giving the impression anyway of thinking. A man with a donkey-load of melons came by. The sergeant stopped him and bought three of the melons, ordering the boy to cut them up and distribute the wedges. Court for the moment was adjourned while the girl, the boy, the "law" — all of us — ate melon.

Proceedings were about to begin again when we saw the three girls coming from the river. The sergeant, the gendarmes, and the boy stood up to watch them. The mother, meanwhile, slipped a breast from her blouse and began to nurse the infant.

I had to be on my way before the case was settled, but certainly the girl got a man or money.

*

People say, "It is so quiet here." It is and yet it isn't. When, for example, the grapes come on, there is heard from all the vineyards the hooting of peasant boys put there to scare the birds away. There are the birds themselves: the whistle of the nightingales at dawn and dusk, the long, lonely call of the owls on autumn evenings, the crows and their nagging caw as they stream back from the fields to nest in the plane trees for the night.

And then the orchard sounds: on full moon nights the whoops of the men carousing in them and the splutter of their drums. Also, but in the daytime, the strange chorus of the women who take a girl to some orchard to celebrate her coming marriage, their high vibratoed ululation — the call, half taunt, half solicitation, of female to maleness, as animal as the cries and whimperings of love.

There are, too, the sounds that come from the village minaret: the thrice daily calls to prayer, the chanting of the Koran's first chapter when someone dies, and, all through the mourning month of Moharram, the singing of litanies to the martyrs — Ali, also called Hezrat-e-Ali, and Ali's son, Hussain. And then blind Akbar. When there is news of general interest — a lost child, the arrival of a performing strong man, a feast to which all are invited — he stands on a village roof and calls it out, and in the silence he can be heard for miles.

The lanes have their sounds as well: the rumble of herds being driven to market, sometimes the shepherd playing his flute. And then, especially on spring and summer nights, a peasant alone, going home, will sing, partly to keep himself company, partly to keep away the spirits of the dark.

Finally there are the sounds of the seasons. The spring winds sough like a distant sea, and this winter we would sometimes hear the long roar of a mountain avalanche or, deep in the night, the snapping of the orchard boughs constricting in the coldness.

So I wonder what we mean when we say that it is quiet here. Perhaps there are two categories, one of things called noise, another of things called sounds, and perhaps the latter do not offend the quietness any more than stones dropped in a pool.

The Hunting Expedition

I HAD TWO FRIENDS, during my time at the Garden, of whom I was very fond. One was an elderly attorney named Mr. Dadgah, the other a grain merchant named Mr. Bazargan.

Mr. Dadgah was a short man with a grand belly and little legs. Due perhaps to the little legs he always stood somewhat canted forward and he walked with a waddle. He had a round, owlish face, wore steel spectacles, and his hair flowed over his ears in thick chestnut wings. On top of his head, both indoors and out, he kept a high-crowned hat. My memory of Mr. Pickwick is not very clear, but Mr. Dadgah made me think of him.

At some point in his youth Mr. Dadgah had considered killing himself. Casting about for a way out, he consulted a man in the town who was known to be wise. The wise man told him to forgo ambition, to expect little, and to live quietly "in a corner of life." Mr. Dadgah had followed this advice, and from his corner, watching, he had developed for other people much humor and tolerance and for himself a code of behavior to which he was quietly but firmly faithful. All in all, it seemed to me that Mr. Dadgah had lived a good and rather happy life.

Mr. Bazargan, Mr. Dadgah's friend, was some years younger, though well on his way to developing the same buckety figure. He was, however, a much softer man in appearance: dimpled, pink, a little languorous, his eyes as gleaming and expectant as a pretty woman's. Yet there was good bone beneath that softness, for he was a shrewd merchant and also the responsible head of an enormous family, a trick in Iran as it is anywhere else. His house in the bazaar quarter of the town contained his children, wives, mother, brothers, nephews and nieces, and sisters-in-law — some fifty people in all. It was, I believe, this admirable combination of traits — his repose and gentleness together with his ability, when necessary, to be resolute and swift — which made me like him, even envy him.

Mr. Dadgah, Mr. Bazargan, and I were shooting companions. In the autumn and early spring we often took a half day and went off to the hills. Mr. Dadgah was well accoutered for these excursions. He wore good tweeds and gaiters and his gun and cartridge cases were of the finest English leather. Mr. Bazargan was less elegant, but he carried the best of guns and also the brandy flask.

Mr. Dadgah, on reaching our destination, would invariably announce that it was too early or too late for the birds to be *really* flying, and so we would lay a carpet in a hollow and settle down to a game of cards and frequent pulls from the brandy flask. The truth of the matter is that, except for a few perfunctory volleys, we never shot at all on these excursions but passed our time in talking, drinking, and cheating at cards. This could not have suited me better. I like to shoot but I prefer to do so alone. My pleasure in these outings was simply the pleasure which I took in my companions and in being out under the sky.

One evening in late spring Mamdali announced that Mr. Dadgah had come to call. I went out to the gallery to find him puffing up the steps more quickly than usual, smiling, too, more broadly than usual, and so I knew that something was up, something pleasant. Sitting down, his arms folded across his belly, his head stuck out at me like an old turtle, he stated his news. He had come to propose not one of our pedestrian half days in the field but in-

stead a full-scale, three-day "expedition" — and his eyebrows flew up as he uttered this impressive word. The
plan came out.

Mr. Dadgah knew two brothers who lived in a valley
halfway down to the gulf. This valley was a veritable zoo
and bird park all in one: the sport would be excellent.
Mr. Bazargan had business with the brothers —
something to do with the purchase of wheat — and with
another farmer, too, who lived in the area. Also, Mr.
Dadgah had certain legal matters to discuss with a man in
a town on the way to the valley. So an expedition would
combine business and pleasure, as activities in Iran often
do. Finally, Mr. Dadgah announced — winking both his
eyes at me, a habit of his when life promised to be particularly droll and sweet — this expedition would be an occasion for us "to go out and see the world!" and he
winked again and flung out his hand at the perfection of
it all.

Several days later, at five in the morning, we met to
start out on our expedition. There were many delays.
First of all, Mr. Dadgah was dissatisfied with the way the
servants had loaded the car. Everything had to be taken
out and put in again: the baskets of fruit, two caldrons of
rice, presents for our hosts (albums with painted covers),
an armory of guns, carpets, bedrolls, bolsters, a hamper
of vodka and wine, bags of raisins and nuts, a backgammon board. The last reminded Mr. Dadgah that he had
forgotten the playing cards, and it took some time to find
where in his house he had hidden them — for his wife, a
ferociously devout old woman, disapproved of gambling.
The cards found, we were ready at last.

It had been decided before leaving that for reasons of
"safety" we would travel in a caravan. Mr. Dadgah had
not lived for long in the modern Iran of safe roads. Dur-

ing most of his life any journey had held the threat of brigands and the rapacious tribes, and he had not forgotten. Accordingly we were traveling with two cars: myself, Mr. Bazargan, Mr. Dadgah, and the latter's nephew Hussain, a boy in his twenties, in one; the servants plus our gear and provisions in the other.

And so we started out, stopping three times, however, before leaving the town. Mr. Dadgah had forgotten his laxative powders, Mr. Bazargan, his flute, and then there was Mr. Dadgah's stop to buy more cartridges for, as he said, "We shall be swamped with game." At nine o'clock our expedition passed through the town's south gate.

We were on the road no more than ten minutes when Mr. Dadgah signaled out the window with his handkerchief and our caravan drew up at a teahouse. It seemed rather early for a break, but after we had gathered inside I realized its purpose. Our expedition could not begin without being signalized in some fashion, without, as it were, some brief rite of inauguration. Mr. Dadgah recited a prayer for the protection of travelers, Mr. Bazargan gave us a poem on the joys of journeys, and we all exchanged our speculations on what the next three days might hold for us. Then Mr. Dadgah cleared his throat and lifted his great bottom slightly off the bench, at the same time lifting his hat. It was an indication that he wished to make an important announcement.

"With your permission, I would like to suggest a few rules for our journey. Drivers will keep their eyes off the village girls for otherwise, distracted, they may plunge us into a ditch. Wrestling will be confined to back seats. [Iranian men tussle with each other to the end of their lives.] Alms will be given to all beggars and further I would suggest a brief stop at all wayside shrines. Does anyone have recommendations to add to these?"

Mr. Bazargan raised his hand. "We must stop and loiter whenever we wish: to make tea, a fine view, a swim perhaps, the calls of nature of course."

"Quite," replied Mr. Dadgah. "Haste is the work of the devil." In the spirit of the proverb another round of tea was ordered. The tea finished, Mr. Dadgah clapped his knees and said, "Yah Ali" ("Praise Ali"). We got up and went out to the cars. Finally, really, at last, we were off on our expedition.

The road was a very old one. Pliny, writing in the first century, called it "the thousand steps." And indeed one could still see parts of the old caravan route with its switchback stairways of rock ascending the mountain walls. The present road, a rock-strewn ledge blasted from the mountainside, drops precipitously four thousand feet to the gulf and is dangerously narrow, often no wider than a car. Looking around, one felt in a sea tossed by tidal waves, the raging snow-topped mountain peaks, the blue abysses. These were usually our views, but sometimes there would come into sight the white tower of a gendarme fort, flag flying, and sometimes too — that mark of the Iranian countryside — the green bloom of a tile-domed shrine.

So we bowled along, no parapet between us and the thousand-foot drops, my companions unconcerned, having given themselves up to the will of God, myself drawing every sinew tight as we swung out and around the rims of the curves. Mr. Dadgah, offering the bag of nuts, began to tell us tales of his boyhood when he traveled the road on horseback. Slapping both knees and blinking his eyes, he went into much detail about a night he and some friends had spent with a gypsy girl on the outskirts of a village.

"You were most profligate in your youth," Mr. Bazargan said, winking at me.

"Of course," replied Mr. Dadgah, "what else is youth for, just as age is for prayer. And speaking of prayer, look down." We did and saw below us a small plain with a shrine to one side of it, the finial of the dome sparking light as if sending us a message. "Since it stands by our road we shall stop here and pay our respects. Do you know, by the way, the history of this plain?" I told him I did not. "It's known for two things: its lions, and its wild narcissus. I regret to say that we are late for both. The narcissus bloomed six months ago, the last lion was shot when I was a boy. But they used to come down in great numbers to play and hunt in the plain. In fact, there is a story —," and he tapped Mr. Bazargan in the front seat to listen. "They say that Hezrat-e-Ali once came to this plain — of course he was never in Iran — and being tired he sat down under a tree to sleep. When he woke what do you think he saw — a lion coming toward him. But the lion held in his teeth a sheaf of narcissus and he dropped these at Ali's feet." Mr. Dadgah fluttered his fingers. "Of course it's only a story — but still —"

By now we had descended to the plain. It felt so good to be there for the simple reason that one could not fall off it. A chalky road ran through the turf and to either side were willows, their whips swiping the car as we passed along. Ahead, to the right, stood the shrine, a sad-looking little building, settled askew on one haunch, its dome tipped like a rakish hat.

"Halt, halt!" cried Mr. Dadgah as we neared the shrine gate, and his nephew, Hussain, drew up and stopped.

"This shrine," Mr. Dadgah said, "contains a stone bearing the hoof-print of Ali's horse."

"But I thought you said — " I began, and then dropped it, remembering that my logic was not appropriate.

We stooped in under the door to find the stone enclosed in an iron grill at the center of the little room and bearing a horse's hoof-print. Mr. Dadgah raised his hat and then knelt to kiss the grill. He rose unsteadily, patting his belly.

"Thank God the Prophet enjoined these obeisances, for otherwise this thing," he patted his belly again, "would be quite out of bounds."

Outside we found that the servants had set up the samovar under a willow, and so we all lay down on the turf to take our tea.

"I could stay here all morning," Mr. Bazargan said.

"But the hunt!" Mr. Dadgah countered, and we finally gathered ourselves together. At the gate Mr. Dadgah put a bill in the contribution box. "Someone will probably steal it," he said, "but no doubt someone who needs it. It all comes to the same thing in the end."

At the far side of the plain we dropped again, the road spiraling down into another of the plunging blue abysses. Beyond this rose a high range of mountains, their slopes yellow in the sun, the draws blue-black with shadow.

"In those mountains," said Hussain, mischief in his eyes, "is the pass of Baba Abbas. We shall have some fun with him."

"We shall not!" said Mr. Dadgah. "The very idea. We shall stop and nothing — untoward — will happen, I trust." And what might be "untoward," I asked. Egged on by Mr. Bazargan, and despite Mr. Dadgah's protests, Hussain explained. Baba Abbas was a beggar who stood at the pass in the mountains waiting for travelers to give alms to him as a kind of payoff to God for a safe descent. This is a common practice in Iran, but Baba Abbas was no common beggar. If travelers did not appear to be slowing down in order to stop and give him money, he would insult them by dropping his pants and exposing himself.

"Disgraceful," said Mr. Dadgah. "This country. We Iranians. May God have mercy on us. And people think that it is funny," he said, glowering at Mr. Bazargan and Hussain. He flung himself back in his seat and looked out the window. "As if the world weren't ugly enough without looking at some old man's private parts. My God!" He leaned forward and tapped Hussain on the shoulder. "You will remember to stop at the pass so that we may give Baba some money and thus avoid this — unseemly display." Hussain did not answer.

By now we had reached the bottom of the drop and were in a small village. The houses, stair-stepped up the yellow flanks of the mountains, were of the usual clay and had flat roofs of brush topped with a crust of plaster. Each house projected to the south a balcony almost as big as itself, making the place look more like a village of balconies than a village of houses. We drove below them, along a narrow, jogging lane. In one of the jogs someone had painted, blue and crude as tattoos, a scene of crowned figures hunting. Mr. Dadgah explained that centuries before the place had been a royal preserve and that the men of the village were still famous as hunters.

On the outskirts of this village one of the farmers lived with whom Mr. Bazargan had business, so we drew up. At the doorway of the long, low, brush-topped house stood a hump of a figure in a blue-checked chador — the farmer's wife. Bowing low in the old fashion, she ushered us in and led us to a room laid with carpets and bolsters, with French doors giving out on a barren courtyard. The farmer himself immediately came in, a strong, weathered old fellow with red, knotted cheeks and blue eyes gone pale and a little wet. He propelled us to some blankets at the end of the room, the place of honor, while he, to show his respect for us, sat down in the doorway. His wife stood behind him, leaning against the doorjamb, flapping her chador across her face like a fan, taking us in.

The usual courtesies were exchanged, the declarations of respect and faithfulness, everyone with his hand across his heart and bowing. Then came talk of crops and weather and of the farmer's family — he had seven sons. As we talked, four of the sons, barefoot, in wide, swinging trousers, came through the French doors bringing tea and fruit — bulls of boys, heavy-calfed, big-torsoed. Yet, as they each went down on one knee to serve the refreshments, they were as graceful as elegant Jesuits before a high altar.

"Ma sha'allah" ("God is great"), said Mr. Dadgah. "Such fine, strong sons." The farmer threw out his hand deprecatingly.

"The seed was indifferent but the ground," and he jerked his head in the direction of the old woman, "— ah, the ground was very rich." The old woman closed the chador across her face, her shoulders shaking, and she laughingly muttered something which we couldn't catch. It occurred to me, as it had before with such people, that the seeding of crops and the seeding of offspring, the harvesting of both, was for them much the same thing.

It was now time for business. Mr. Bazargan went over and sat down cross-legged beside the farmer, and their heads went together to discuss the crops and their purchase. We, meanwhile, drank more tea and joked with one of the sons, who was to marry soon.

Mr. Bazargan's business finished, we made ready to go.

The farmer insisted, however, that we see his orchard, and so we went out and across the courtyard to look at the trees. He touched each of them as he went along. This was the oldest, from an earlier orchard, that was the heaviest bearer, a third he singled out for its graceful shape, and so on, discussing each tree as he might have discussed his sons.

They all came out to wish us goodbye — the old man, his wife, and now all seven sons — standing there in front of their low, strong house.

"What a fortunate man," said Mr. Dadgah, as we drove away.

The road continued level for a little while and then, in a series of loops, began the ascent to the pass of Baba Abbas. In the hollow of one of the loops lay a graveyard. Iranian graveyards ordinarily contain no headstones, for religious law dictates that markers must not cast a shadow and thus the graves are outlined with nothing more than a low rim of bricks. But exceptions are sometimes made, the Iranians even in death liking to transgress, and in this graveyard there was one of these exceptions, a small stone lion, signifying that there lay a man who had been strong and brave, a great hunter perhaps.

It was an irony that just as we passed the lion a flock of pigeons flew up from behind a wall.

"Halt, halt!" cried Mr. Dadgah. "Our first game!" And out came the guns, poking from every window, volley after volley discharged into the scattering flight of wings. A single pigeon dropped to the ground. "Well," said Mr. Dadgah, "it is a beginning at any rate. We were not really prepared and shall do better next time, I trust."

"Perhaps," said Mr. Bazargan. "But I would feel more certain if we had left the vodka, backgammon board, and cards at home."

"Nonsense, Mr. Bazargan," replied Mr. Dadgah. "This is no half-day lark in the hills. This is an *expedition*. No, once we reach the field and get ourselves organized it will be, I assure you, a veritable slaughter. In fact —," but he stopped, for now we were approaching the pass of Baba Abbas. "Hussain," he leaned forward and tapped his nephew's shoulder. "Now remember. We must stop for Baba Abbas."

"We shall stop," said Hussain. Yet he didn't slow down. Ahead on the level stretch of the pass we could see a figure in the road — Baba Abbas, I assumed. The car sped on.

"Slow down, Hussain, SLOW DOWN, I command you!" cried Mr. Dadgah. But on we went. Just before we reached it, the figure in the road skipped aside. "My God!" exclaimed Mr. Dadgah. And indeed there was Baba Abbas, his pants down, wagging his tool at us. The brakes went on and we skidded to a stop just short of him.

"I have stopped," said Hussain.

"Your father was a dog," replied Mr. Dadgah. Then he rolled down the window. "Come here, sir," he called to the beggar. "Have you no shame, sir?" The old man ambled over, hitching his trousers up.

"I am starving to death," said the beggar. "What would you have me do? Would you prefer a gun?"

"Starving!" said Mr. Dadgah. "With your odious blackmail you've more money in the sock than all of us put together. Nonetheless, here," and he gave the beggar a bill. "At least have the decency to buy yourself some underpants." Then he rolled up the window. "And you," he said, hitting Hussain on the head with the bag of nuts, "— you disgrace to your father." But he turned to me and said in a low voice, "My word, the old fellow was thick. Must do well with the gypsy women. Which reminds me. . . ." and off he went on some detail, which he had forgotten to tell us, about his night with the gypsy girl.

It was almost noon and Mr. Dadgah and Mr. Bazargan, both of whom had large, insistent appetites, were peering ahead for the bridge near which we were to lunch. The carload of servants had already been sent ahead to set up a camp for us, lay the carpets, unpack the food, and get the braziers going.

Finally, the bridge came into view, broadside to us, one of those simple, handsome bridges so common in Iran. This one had two slightly humped spans meeting midway at a natural plinth of rock, the other ends of the spans joining the cliffs as if grafted, the brick and stone tongue-and-grooved together.

At the opposite end of the bridge stood the servants' car. This surprised us, for the servants should have been by the river bank putting our camp in order. But as we drove up to the car, we saw a man leaning against it who turned out to be a friend of Mr. Dadgah's. This gentleman, a Mr. Yazdan, was staying, he told us, at a pavilion down the river. Passing our camp, he had recognized the servants, and now he had come to invite us to join him and his friends.

"A most agreeable turn of affairs, Mr. Yazdan," said Mr. Dadgah, and so we started out along a track which followed the river and led to the pavilion.

We came at last to a mill, as far as we could go by car. I hoped that it might be here that we would picnic. The mill, bowered in willows, was tucked into a bend in the river, and the place was pleasantly noisy with its whistling wheel and the cries of *lak-lak*, as storks are called in Iran. But it seemed that the picnic was to be at the pavilion itself, which stood on the opposite bank. We crossed the glistening river on a footbridge of peeled poplar poles and entered a field of wheat. The pavilion lay downstream a few yards, set in a slope of orchard above the river bank.

It was the usual affair: on the ground level there was a room for storing tools and fruit and stabling for a donkey, outside a stairway led up to a big balcony with a wrought iron railing, and at the rear of this, through French doors, there was a plain white room with carpets and a fireplace. It was, Mr. Yazdan said, the "country house" of a doctor friend of his who lived in the village, a fifteen-minute walk away.

Introductions were made. Mr. Yazdan's party consisted of relatives — brothers, uncles, and cousins. We settled down on the carpets, while the servants prepared the lunch out on the terrace. Mr. Yazdan poured us some of the local wine, cherry-colored stuff with a minty, fresh flavor, and, pointing to a side of lamb hanging in the doorway, insisted that we share their kabob when it was ready. It soon was, and we moved out to the long, white cloth spread on the terrace. It was set — each setting simply a round of flat bread — with twenty places. The food was brought on: kabobs, plates of herbs and greens, chickens in rice, big pitchers of yogurt water, the cherry wine. We left our talk and ate.

The view from the terrace was a refreshing one in the full sense of the word. Saint Francis once said that God must be praised for having created both thirst and water; he may be praised as well for having created in Iran both deserts and oases. After our long morning in the barren mountains, the view down the valley was as quenching as the coldest water. In a long, glinting loop, the river ran between the paddies of spring wheat that covered the valley floor and spread back into the coves and bays of the mountain line. Here and there, as blurred as mirages, rose stands of silver poplar; and there were pockets, too, in the protected places, of cherry and almond. Down perhaps a mile from us, on the far side, the mountains projected a peninsula of black rock into the green of the valley floor, and on the crest of this stood the village. It looked like El Greco's Toledo, the walls rising in sheer brown shafts from the rock up to a towered citadel. A little below stood the village gate, a great black keyhole in the brown ramparts. From the valley, a ribbon of road led up to it.

My mind, with the road, went through the gate and into the village, and I began to imagine the good life the villagers lived, there above their beautiful valley. Mr. Dadgah must have caught the meaning of my dreaming look, for he put his hand on my knee and said, "It could not be more perfect — except. It was only a month ago that I was called in on a case: a man brought from this valley to the town. He had no head. Some fight over water. No, my dear," and he patted my knee, "there are no Edens." And I was reminded that the word *romantic*, as applied to a person, does not exist in Iranian, nor does its opposite, *realist*. No Iranian would so limit his sense of the world by being one or the other.

We were getting up now from the cloth. A few of the others had already gone to the river bank and we joined them, lying down in some freshly plowed furrows, our backs against the ridges. To our left stood a planting of young poplars which moved like plumes in the breeze from the river, dappling the furrows and us with shadow. In front of us, noisy and fast, ran the water, slate grey, except in the shallows where it ran silver. Now and then people would cross the bridge — slow-striding peasants in their swinging trousers, leading a donkey weighed down

with nets of clover, blue-hooded women, children hopping, an old man with a staff.

Drowsily we mumbled to each other until a cousin of
Mr. Yazdan's, a tall and gaunt young army officer, stood
up to play his flute. He was wearing blue-striped winter
underwear which clung to his thighs and calves, and
small, finely made black shoes. With one leg crooked,
and with his emaciated, rather insolent face, he looked
like a bullfighter. Curling his upper lip to one side, as a
dog snarls, he mouthed the end of the flute to get it going — the notes then coming, breathy and inexact — and
began to pace the furrow, his head swinging a little to the
line of the melody. Hussain was crouching down on the
ridge of the furrow with his drum between his thighs, and
he began to snap his fingers along the skin. A voice from
the poplar grove, where some of the party were stretched
out on carpets, answered the flute in its pauses with a
shrill, lamenting cry; then the flute and the drum would
mellowly resume, reassuring, as it were, the crying singer.
For a time the dialogue went on, the plea and the answer,
but finally, as if nothing could be resolved, no true answer
given, the flute abruptly stopped, and the young officer
slumped down against a tree trunk and closed his eyes to
nap. But the drummer, perhaps not wanting the mood to
end in apathy, snapped out a series of high notes which
splattered against the silence like gravel thrown at glass.

Mr. Dadgah had come to sit beside me, reclining back
on the ridge, the rise of his belly cutting off the view of
the bridge. Tipping his hat down over his eyes, he gestured at the men around us — some sleeping, others shar-
ing a water pipe, two boys doing tumbling tricks on a long
strip of carpet.

"You know," he began, "we are a terrible people, we
Iranians — thieves, mountebanks, rascals. How dis-

pleased God must be with us. And yet there is one thing. Today, any day in spring or summer, should God look down he would see the scraps of carpet, like that one, laid all over our land, on the mountain slopes and by the rivers, on the rooftops and in the orchards, little groups of men, and of women, tasting the air, receiving the sun, relishing all this which he in his kindness has given us. And surely in this he must be pleased with us, don't you think? I believe so," he said without waiting for my answer. "I hope so. For otherwise," he laughed, "hell will be filled with Iranians — and speaking of hell, that's where our host for tonight will wish us if we don't get started." He sat up and clapped his hands. "Come, come," he called to the others. "We have lolled enough." With much stretching and yawning we got our things together and, thanking Mr. Yazdan and his party, we started out across the bridge.

Once back on the main road we began yet another descent. This would lead us to the "hot country," as Iranians call it, the land below the plateau, where there are palms and the air is muggy. We could see in the distance the first of the palms and could already feel a softness in the air, prelude to the later heaviness. But for now it was pleasant, and we rolled down all the windows to let it flow around us.

"The winds of spring are good for the body," said Mr. Dadgah.

My companion in the back seat for this part of the journey was Mr. Bazargan, Mr. Dadgah having gone to the front so that he might, as he explained, keep a sharp eye out for game. Mr. Bazargan and I, a box of cookies between us, began to talk about other journeys we had taken in other places. For him, I described fishing jaunts in Oregon and a bike trip along the Devon coast, and he told me of his pilgrimage to Mecca and also of a long trip all around Iran which he had made as a boy with friends.

"I do not know," he said, "if it is the custom in your country, but here young men will sometimes find a girl to take along with them on a journey. And we did that, disguising her as a boy," he threw his hand out, "not to cause scandal."

"Hah," said Mr. Dadgah, from the front seat, "and you accuse me of having been profligate!"

"We were all profligate," replied Mr. Bazargan. "As you say, 'youth' — and the other things, worse, that go with youth," he ended with sudden seriousness, and turned to me again. "On our first day out we stopped to picnic in country rather like this," he motioned out the window. "After we had eaten and rested, the girl stood up — she was barefoot, in trousers and shirt, and she had taken her cap off and her hair poured down — and she told us that if we gave her a head start, she would run up into the hills, and that whoever caught her could have her. Imagine! It excited us so — we were boys, five of us — and we clapped her on the back for having such a good idea. So off she went. In those days," he tapped his belly, "I was slim and fast and above all I wanted her very much. But she was faster, like a gazelle — how she could leap! The other lads finally used up their wind — most of it trying to trip each other — but I went on, half of me dying but the other half, the lower half, wanting to go on." He laughed. "I was like a young stallion across a field after a mare. Finally, I caught up with her or perhaps," he stroked his jaw and gave me a sidewise smile, "she slowed down for me. We stayed the whole afternoon making love."

"A most agreeable adventure," said Mr. Dadgah.

"Oh, but that's not the end of it — the sad end of it,"

replied Mr. Bazargan. "By the time the journey was over, I was in love with the girl. I don't mean with the idea of marriage — that was out of the question — but still, love. Then a strange, an unpleasant, thing happened. I curse myself to this day. At the time of the trip I was wearing a ring which had brought me much luck. She wanted it, would tease me for it, and at last I gave it to her. But as soon as I did, I realized that I had given my luck away and I wanted it back. We began to struggle — it was the last day of the journey and we were off in some woods — and what did the creature do but swallow it. I hit her then, angry, for I wanted my luck back. And I got it. The blow made the poor child sick, or perhaps it was the hurt of my meanness, and she brought the ring up. Picking it out of the vomit, she gave it to me and then went away."

"Awk," said Mr. Dadgah. "It is very ugly. All of it, your action and hers. It's a story for a dark and mournful day. Not for our expedition," and he turned in his seat and looked at Mr. Bazargan with sadness, the closest thing to reproach that I had ever seen on his face.

"I know," said Mr. Bazargan. "You must forgive me. But these hills — they reminded me so much."

"And the ring?" asked Mr. Dadgah.

"I put it away in a chest and it is there today."

"And the girl?"

"God knows. Perhaps at the end of her days in some whorehouse, perhaps married, perhaps dead. But I would do much to find her, for now — may God have mercy on me — I would give her the ring and much else."

"Yes," said Mr. Dadgah. No more was said, and for a little while we rode along in silence.

By now dusk was coming on, for we had lingered late at our picnic. The horizon was a band of red, the mountains looming and black — an empty world except for a gendarme fort on a spur a few miles to our left, a tower at each of its corners, its walls a chalky pink. The only movement was a flapping flag and the black figure of a gendarme, his coat rising like a cloak in the wind as he ran along the parapet.

"It is unwise," said Mr. Dadgah, "to be on the road at night."

"If we hurry along," said Mr. Bazargan, "we can reach Aliabad not more than an hour after nightfall, but there is danger in that, too — hurrying on a road like this. May I suggest, Mr. Dadgah, that we stop for the night at the first teahouse?" It was agreed.

But no teahouse appeared. On and on we drove, the darkness falling fast, until finally it was night. Mr. Dadgah took out his gold watch and his money and buried both in the bag of nuts.

"It is as well to be prepared," he said. As he said this, we saw far below us a light, one light, indicating a teahouse and not a village. Down we went until the light appeared to be no more than a few hundred yards ahead of us. But there was an obstacle. After coming around a curve, we saw below us a river, sliding and oily, like a great reptile in the moonlight, and there was no bridge. We drove up close to illuminate the water with our headlights, for we knew we would have to ford it, but the light showed nothing of its depth, only a fast current with crests to it. We got out and walked to the bank and began to lob stones into the water to gauge its depth. It was not as shallow as we would have liked, but there was no alternative to crossing it.

Hussain roared the motor and we started out. Midway the motor spluttered and stopped. Looking back, we saw the servants getting out of their car and preparing to wade in to come to our aid. At the same time, we heard hollering from the other bank and saw figures striding out in the water toward us.

"What are these?" asked Mr. Dadgah. And indeed they were a wild-looking crew, their chests bare, an unusual thing to see in Iran, and their features crowded in on their faces as the features are crowded on a dog or a monkey. "They must be Arabs," said Mr. Dadgah in an undertone, "for after all we are near the gulf. But no, that isn't fair, for the Arabs, with all their faults, have the grand faces of hawks. Then thieves, perhaps." Meanwhile the men, whoever they were, were doing a very good job, with the help of the servants, of getting us going. With much straining and calls on the aid of Hezrat-e-Ali, we finally began to move. At the bank Hussain tried the motor again, and it caught. We drove up onto the land.

"You have been most kind," Mr. Dadgah said, peering closely at the strange-looking men. They babbled back in some dialect which I didn't understand.

By now the servants had, without mishap, forded the stream, and we set out for the teahouse escorted by the "monkey men," as Mr. Dadgah whisperingly referred to them. The teahouse, back under the trees, flared by a pressure lamp, looked like a cave. There hung from the lintel one of those strange cat's-cradle frameworks of colored seeds which are believed to repel the evil eye. We could smell rue burning, too, also to ward off the evil spirits. Beyond the doorway the teahouse keeper sat cross-legged on top of his railed pay booth — a heavy, drowsy, whitish man, curled there like a great slug and looking at us out of eyes pushed to slits by the folds of his face.

"Where on earth are we?" Mr. Dadgah whispered.

"Such people! I think we have been bewitched and are in the land of God-knows-where." But then there came dancing toward us out of the depths of the teahouse a smiling old man in a green turban and a ragged gold-buttoned ship steward's jacket. Sliding into a bow, like a cavalier in a minuet, he bade us an elaborate and cheery welcome. We felt once again that we were in the land of the living.

The old fellow scrambled to take our bedrolls and other luggage, throwing them in a heap, and then began furiously to pump the pressure lamp. In the rising light we saw where we were: an earthen floor, adobelike ledges around the wall where bedrolls might be spread, a ceiling of reed matting and poplar poles. We proceeded to settle in, taking off our trousers to be at ease in pajamas and opening a bottle of vodka. Mr. Dadgah ordered some food to supplement our own, though first asking to see the meat.

"I would not," he said to me, "put it past that teahouse keeper to give us dog." The old man in the green turban came back with the meat, holding it to Mr. Dadgah's nose to sniff.

"It is very beautiful meat," the old man said, "and I will kabob it for you as I would for a bride."

Sitting back cross-legged on our bedrolls, we ate like gluttons and pulled at the vodka. The teahouse keeper dozed off, now and then hiccuping, his great body jerking up, and then subsiding again. The old servant squatted on his haunches in front of us, his turban now very much over one eye from all his exertions. He asked us the usual questions — where we were from, where we were going, what we did — and then he began to tell us about himself. He was, he said, a "retired pirate" from the gulf, and his name was "Captain" Abul. The "damned British" with their gun boats had driven him off the water, and that plus other bad luck had forced him into his present position.

"The world is a witch," he said, quoting from an Iranian poem.

"You deserve the witch," said Mr. Dadgah. "Men seldom pay for their sins, but it seems you are doing so," and, laughing, he clapped the old fellow on the back.

Finally, orders were given to turn down the lamp. After a brief bout of shenanigans — Mr. Dadgah received a pillow in his face — we went off to sleep.

At five the next morning, and to shouts from the pirate of, "Rise for God has given us the day," we got up and went out to the teahouse garden to do our ablutions, washing our faces and combing our hair at the mirrors that hung on nails in the tree trunks. Mr. Dadgah, rubbing his hands with orange leaves to perfume and oil them, told the pirate to step lively and bring us breakfast. In a moment it was laid out under a trellis, a bowered place with a brass samovar the size of a washtub and, hanging from one of the poplar supports, a large oleograph of Empress Maria Theresa, bosomy and pink. We ate honey, cheese, and bread, enjoying the teahouse garden and happy at the end of it all that we had been obliged to make this forced stop.

By seven — for Mr. Dadgah and Mr. Bazargan wanted a game of backgammon before starting off — we were ready to leave. As we went out the gate, the pirate caught up with us and, with his courtly glide, presented me with a bracelet of threaded almonds.

"A gift for our guest," he said, "here in the hot country and from such a faraway place." Mr. Dadgah and the others of our party all gravely bowed, thanking him, while I to complement, in a sense to complete, this little gesture, reached in my pocket for a good tip. We drove off, the pirate saluting in fine naval fashion, even the slug of a teahouse keeper languidly flapping his hand at us.

Within an hour we had reached Aliabad, the town that lay near the valley for which we were bound. It looked so different from the plateau towns, spread out like a suburb, the houses white and set amongst palms. It was a holiday, the birthday of the Prophet. On the main street the merchants, decorating for the occasion, had swagged unrolled bolts of dress material, as though it were bunting, across the facades of their shops. From the minaret of the mosque a loudspeaker blared verses from the Koran. We passed beneath a scaffold arch draped with carpets and mirrors, pictures of the Prophet and Ali at its apex. There were crowds everywhere, the dark, nervous faces of the gulf.

The house of Mr. Dadgah's client stood in the bazaar quarter. We went through big gates, down an alley of palms, and drew up before a heavy block of a house. Our host, Mr. Abbasi, sat at a tea table under the vaults of the veranda, fanning himself with a palm leaf. He rose as soon as he recognized us and came across the gravel drive, a hulk of a man, very sporty in white linen and a blue ascot. We piled out, Mr. Dadgah profusely apologizing for our late arrival. Mr. Abbasi, after kissing Mr. Dadgah on both cheeks and shaking hands with the rest of us, led us to the veranda, where he hit a gong for a servant to bring more chairs. Then he began jokingly to chastise us for missing the gazelle he had prepared the night before in expectation of our visit.

Tea, fruit, and other refreshments were served. After a decent interval, Mr. Dadgah and Mr. Abbasi retired to a room in the house, while we stretched out our legs and relaxed on the veranda. Blossoming vines walled one end of it and water dripped down through the vines from a trough on the roof. Now and then a light breeze would pass through the vines, blowing the perfume of the blossoms and the coolness of the water across to us.

While we waited for Mr. Dadgah's business to be concluded, his friends, the two brothers from the valley, arrived. It had been arranged that they would meet us there. We were introduced. Malek Sohrab, in his early forties, was a tall, gangly, chagrined-looking man. His brother, Malek Rostam, was a brute with a short thick neck, black hair curling low on his brow and nape, and rolling, half-mad, black eyes. They were both dressed in country clothes, the loose black trousers and wide brass-buckled belts.

I had heard something about the brothers from Mr. Dadgah. Their father had been literally king of the valley, entirely ignoring the central government and its demands for such things as taxes and conscripts. Finally, in the late 1930s, Reza Shah had had the valley bombed and the brothers, the father now dead, submitted. It was said they still smarted under the humiliation. Of the two brothers, Malek Rostam in particular was well known, especially for his violence and strength. There were stories that he could support a jeep on his shoulders and that now and then, putting on a coat and tie, he would go off to Tehran to amuse himself by smashing up cafes and clubs.

Presently Mr. Dadgah and Mr. Abbasi returned to the veranda. Greetings were exchanged. Mr. Abbasi served some of his home-brewed date liquor. A toast was drunk to the coming hunt. And then we piled into the cars again and started out for our camp.

The valley of our destination was, in its way, a famous one. From the fourth to the seventh century it had been a capital for a dynasty called the Sassanians. Though warriors, off battling most of their lives with the Romans and the Byzantines, they nonetheless found time to create a vigorous, interesting civilization — one in which such things as polo, chess, a good cuisine, hunting, and music played important parts; and which, in silver, silk, and stone, produced a handsome art. Now little was left besides the valley itself, and its bas-reliefs.

As we passed out of the desert glare and through the break in the mountain walls, I began to understand why the Sassanian kings had chosen the place. It was more a crevasse than a valley, for both sides were bordered by sheer cliffs; yet there was no darkness, the air yellow with sun. Low trees and grass covered the floor of the place, water glinting everywhere through them — it was the river, shallow and spreading, with almost the whole of the valley its bed. To either side, hacked into the yellow rock of the valley walls, there were six or seven great rectangular tableaux of more than life-sized playing-card kings, heraldic figures, massive and boastful, posed in the triumph of war or the glory of the chase. Above and circling them were the blue crowns of the mountains.

We drove along a track between the river and the cliffs, reaching, about halfway up the valley, our camp. It lay below one of the tableaux in a circle of boulders. There were bedrolls against the boulders, shotguns and rifles poking up from the crevices between them, and in the boulder-enclosed hollow a carpet had been laid, a big silver tray set with tea glasses in silver holders at one end of it. A half-dozen men were waiting for us, slumped on their spines against the bedrolls, smoking, cartridge belts loose at their waists. On the incline below, an Arab stallion was staked and here, too, were the brothers, hands on their hips, waiting to receive us.

"You must forgive this camp," Malek Sohrab, the tall brother, said in his rather embarrassed way. Then he went and, stooping, picked up the silver tray, waiting there with it while we came into the circle of the boulders. Malek Rostam, taking Mr. Dadgah's hand, led us to the carpet. The other men now got to their feet and the introductions were made. They were friends and retainers of the brothers — their court. When we had settled ourselves against the boulders, Malek Rostam made a short speech of formal welcome. Mr. Dadgah responded. Then Malek Sohrab came forward with the silver tray. They had put on it, along with the tea, nosegays of the local wild flowers for us to sniff as we took our tea.

Lunch soon followed: gazelle, lamb, and chicken, two kinds of pilau, spinach cakes, wild rhubarb, yogurt and herbs, whiskey, brandy, and the local date spirits. Mr. Dadgah, finishing this huge repast, fell back on his bedroll and stroked his belly.

"Our dear hosts," he said, addressing Mr. Bazargan and me, "have suggested that after a short nap we proceed to the hunt. But I wonder," and he looked at each of us in turn, "did you get enough sleep in that wretched teahouse? Perhaps instead of a short rest you would prefer a long nap?" Looking at his dull eyes, we agreed that a long nap might be in order.

"And you may hunt tonight," said Malek Sohrab. "In fact you might find it more interesting, for we do our night hunting with a gong and torches, the sound and light mesmerizing the beasts."

"It is preferable," said Mr. Dadgah. He stood up, tottering a little, and ordered the servants to spread the bedrolls in the shadow of the boulders. Soon we were asleep.

The chill of late afternoon woke us. Mr. Dadgah and

Mr. Bazargan washed themselves, said their prayers, and then we all helped ourselves from the silver tray. Refreshed by the sleep, the wash, and the tea, Mr. Dadgah proposed to the brothers that they take us on a short tour of the valley. They were agreeable, and so we started out.

We walked along a path that followed the base of the cliffs, coming now and then to one of the bas-reliefs. Before each there was a half-moon pool fed by a spring. These pools, Malek Rostam explained, protected the bas-reliefs from being defaced, and indeed after fifteen centuries they were well preserved. Each showed a Sassanian king, an enormous figure astride a chunky horse, holding in one hand a shield and in the other, a sword. We sat down by one which depicted the subjugation of the Roman Emperor Valerian by Shapur I. The emperor, in his toga, knelt with his head beneath the foot of the king — the king looking like the mailed specter of Hamlet's father.

"They are our ancestors," Malek Rostam said. And looking at him, I saw that indeed he and the figure in the tableau had the same heavy power and pride. "Yet," he continued, "we know almost nothing of them." He turned to me. Since coming to the camp, I had sensed his curiosity about me — a curiosity that struck me as being in part hostile.

"You are educated?" he asked.

"I have been to school," I answered.

"Harvard?"

"No," I said, surprised that he would know the name. "Why Harvard?"

"We have a nephew there," and he grunted, as if it were a disgrace. "He came last summer to hunt with us. They had changed him, of course."

"For better or for worse?" I asked.

"He had the hands of a girl, a thin neck, and his body is

weak. But he speaks well." He passed his hand over his chest. "Perhaps more important in these times. He didn't stay long with us." Then he sighed and looked away.

Mr. Dadgah, listening, swiveled around on the ledge of the pool to face me and Malek Rostam.

"We need each kind of man," he said. "The strong, the learned. Why," he laughed, "we even need merchants, and even sometimes those rascals called lawyers." He pointed to the tableau. "Even in those times they had need of all such men. Though of course," and he ducked his head, looking up at Malek Rostam from under his brows, "the strongest and bravest was king." Then he slapped his knees, stood up, and took Malek Rostam's arm in his own, and we started back for the camp — Malek Rostam once again his swaggering self.

It was nearly dark by the time we got back. A fire was burning in a bay formed by the boulders and it was, as we approached, like a little light show, the figures of the tableau appearing to move and gesticulate in the flickering light. We sat down, waiting for dinner to be prepared. Some of the brothers' men lit pressure lamps and put them here and there, so that we sat in a pool of light edged by the shadows of the boulders, the floor of the pool brilliant with the orange and blue of the carpet. The silver tray came around again, this time bearing little glasses of date spirits, yogurt with herbs, and bread for dunking. The brothers began to tell stories of the old days before the bombings. They had done everything then: collected their own tax from the peasants, sat in judgement in all disputes, trained the boys to fight.

"We tried to rule justly," said Malek Sohrab, "but now!" and he spat. "The shah we believe is a just king, but his servants are knaves," and he spat again.

A mountain sheep, shot in the afternoon while we were

sleeping, was ready now to eat, and we began on it. When I had finished my portion, I had a bone left, which I started to throw off beyond the boulders.

"Wait," said Malek Rostam. "Can you break it?" and he looked at me with a little smile. The bone was about two inches thick, eight inches long. I am not strong, but nonetheless I decided to give it a try. It might have been a bone of steel and I, a butterfly. "Give it to me," said Malek Rostam, and I tossed it to him. He stood up, legs spread, and braced himself against a boulder, his head on his short, thick neck flung back, the eyes gleaming and a little mad like the eyes of a man about to kill or rape. Wrapping a handkerchief around the bone, he grasped it at both ends, brought his knee up under it for leverage, and began to take in deep, increasing pants of breath. Then he bore down, moaning to himself. The shoulders trembled, the cords of the neck jerked out, the eyes bulged; he was like a great engine about to burst with its own power. But the bone didn't break. Shaking his head as though he had received a blow, he rearranged the handkerchief, took a new grasp, and once again the massive shoulders bore down and he moaned like a man at the acme of love. Still the bone didn't break. He stood straight then and with a vicious swing threw the bone against a boulder.

It was an awful moment. The man stripped there before us and no way for him or us to cover his shame. But Mr. Bazargan, who had been leaning back, sleepily observing the scene as though it were all a vanity, instantly sat up and said with a wave of his hand, "But it is impossible to break that bone. No man could do it, there is not enough grasp. Surely, Malek Rostam, you were joking us in even trying." We all grabbed at the excuse. "Impossible" — the word went around the circle. It eased the moment a little but not enough, for Malek Rostam's eyes still had not met our own.

"No," said Mr. Dadgah, "even the man who can bear a jeep on his back," and he inclined his head toward Malek Rostam, "cannot break *that* bone. It's the simple mechanics of the thing. Shapur himself," and he pointed to the tableau, "could not have done such a thing." Malek Rostam finally looked at us. We went on to other subjects then.

It was now getting near the time agreed on for the hunt. And I waited, wondering what ruse Mr. Dadgah would use to avoid or postpone the plan. It came. Now and then during the evening, Mr. Bazargan had practiced a trick which is very common at Iranian outings. He would tickle Mr. Dadgah's ear with a blade of grass, and Mr. Dadgah would slap at himself, thinking it an insect, to everyone's great amusement. Finally, however, Mr. Dadgah was not to be fooled.

"There is an ant in this camp," he said, "and its name is Bazargan."

"But what," said Mr. Bazargan, teasing him, "if it were a snake and you paid no heed?"

"A snake!" cried Mr. Dadgah. "Surely there are no snakes in this valley."

"In fact," said Malek Sohrab, "we are plagued with them. They come in from the desert to get at the water."

"Snakes!" said Mr. Dadgah again. He looked around himself. Mr. Bazargan tickled his ear with the grass and he jumped. "Enough is enough, Mr. Bazargan." Then he stood up. "My dear Malek Rostam and Malek Sohrab," and he bowed to each, "I hate to confess this to you, but I have a mortal fear of snakes. My mother, no doubt, when carrying me —"

"It is nothing," said Malek Sohrab. "Perhaps, instead of

sleeping here for the night, you would prefer to sleep at one of our houses?"

"If it is no inconvenience," said Mr. Dadgah. "This weakness in myself is disgraceful, I know — but I cannot control it." Mr. Bazargan and I, in complicity, rose. The hunt, as usual, had been averted.

So we left the camp and drove up the valley until we came to two great shadowed masses. These were the brothers' houses. We, it was decided, were to be the guests of Malek Rostam. A gate was opened and we went through a barrel vault, across a courtyard, and into a long French-windowed room — the guest quarters. To my surprise, it was elegantly appointed. A fine Isfahan carpet covered the floor, and against one wall there were six bedrolls bound in green silk. On the mantelpiece stood silver candlesticks, a silver bowl, and an envelope of brocade, the wrapping, I knew, for the prayer stone. But the most impressive objects in the room were propped in two arched niches to either side of the fireplace. These were more than life-sized photographs of Malek Rostam framed in wide gilt. One showed him in a homburg, coat, and polka-dot tie; the other, stripped to the waist, shoulders back — a portrait of his strength. I complimented him on the photographs.

"Oh yes," he said gravely, "those are my two lives. I go often, you know, to Tehran. I am received there by important people." I thought of the smashed-up cafes and clubs.

He was an excellent host. Though we protested, he had a light supper served to us, brought magazines, and put candlesticks and jugs of ice water by each of our bedrolls. When he could think of no more to do for us, he ordered a servant to sleep by our door; then, wishing us a good night in his "poor, unworthy house," he left.

The next morning we were awakened by the sunlight shafting through the open French doors. In the courtyard, pitchers, basins, and towels had been set out. Coming back into the room, we sat down against the rolled-up bedrolls, and then a servant placed before each of us a silver tray laid with a folded round of bread, honey, cheese, and tea. While we ate, Malek Rostam, standing in the doorway, outlined for us the entertainments with which he planned to fill our day.

Mr. Dadgah, with many apologies and in the face of strong protests, told Malek Rostam that we would not be able to stay and would, in fact, be leaving within the hour. Mr. Bazargan had an important meeting for the following day, while he himself had a case in court. The brothers — for Malek Sohrab had now come too — protested and even threatened to block the road. Like all country Iranians they considered a visit of no more than one night an insult to their hospitality. Only after Mr. Dadgah had sworn by the Koran that we would come again, and for a longer stay, did they consent to let us go. "But you have deprived us," Malek Rostam added bitterly. I knew that he meant it.

The journey back, like the journey down, was interrupted by many stops. For old times' sake, we paid our respects to the retired pirate and the river bank where we had had our picnic, gave alms to Baba Abbas, briefly called on the farmer with the seven sons, and once again made tea under the willows at the shrine of the hoof-print of Ali's horse.

Once again, too, we stopped at the teahouse on the outskirts of the town. The beginning of the journey had been inaugurated there, so there its successful ending was to be celebrated. We poured the last of the vodka into the tea glasses.

"Let us thank God," said Mr. Dadgah, raising his hat and his big behind. "We have had our hunt," and, laughing, he pointed at the game bag which had contained the single pigeon. "There was other good fortune, too. Mr. Bazargan has bought his wheat at a low price, while I have earned myself a good fee. And then, too," and he turned and smiled at me, "we have seen the world: a proud man humbled, an old one making a disgrace of himself, another blessed with strong, respectful sons. We have seen cowardice," he pointed to himself, "and disobedience," he shook his finger at his nephew Hussain. "And we have seen how God has played with the world, with what caprice and joy he made the mountains and the valleys, the colors he has given them, the water — all for our pleasure, our refreshment." He lifted his glass and we drank. Then we all stood up and shook hands, each of us, as it were, congratulating the other on the happy outcome of the hunting expedition.

Journal II

WHENEVER Khanom makes bread, I go out to the bake-house to eat a piece of it while still warm from the oven. Mamdali made the oven himself. It is a barrel-shaped well, about waist high and sunk into a masonry foundation. The well is constructed of bricks, which he made from earth mixed with water and a little straw, poured into a form, and left to dry in the sun. The interior of the well is smooth-finished. Before making the dough — flour from the mill mixed with water — Khanom builds a small fire in the bottom of the well. When the dough is ready, she forms it into flat rounds which she slaps against the heated wall of the well. It is as simple as that.

This morning, going to the bakehouse for some bread, I found that Mamdali had made Batul a miniature oven and that Khanom was teaching her how to use it. "It is the first and most important thing she must learn," Mamdali said. Batul is four.

That reminded me of something. When Nasair was barely able to walk, Mamdali taught him how to turn the water spigot on and off when his father was watering the garden. Not long after, when Nasair could walk a little better, Mamdali always took him along when spading open or closed the water channels that irrigate the orchard. Water and bread — they are the foundations of life in Iran, and thus the provision of each is the first thing children learn here.

*

The other day I went on a picnic with the children. It was an event, for they rarely go beyond the walls. Nasair wore his high green boots; Batul, her babushka. I carried our lunch in the cartridge bag. They ran ahead of me, squeaking like mice at the things they found: a hole in the lane wall which they said was the house of the "snake king"; a ruined reservoir which they tiptoed past, claiming that a jinni lived there. Once we stopped to look at a little patch of wheat. "What a great field, how spacious!" Nasair said.

But after about ten minutes, their skipping slowed to trudging and they were ready to have their lunch right there in the middle of the lane. I took their hands and joshed them on, for I wanted to eat, and also take a dip, at the pool where the *qanat* comes out. When we reached it, they flopped down with much huffing and puffing, like mountain climbers finally at the summit. What a nice spot it is, the green plate of the pool with the big bell-shaped willows down at one end of it.

We splashed in the pool for a bit and then took our lunch out on a little peninsula of turf. When it was time for tea, we called to join us a goat-herd boy who had been shyly watching through the trees on the far side of the pool. He said nothing in his shyness while drinking his tea, but after finishing he went off and gathered thistle buds and, breaking them open, gave us the pods. We salted the pods and ate them.

On the way back, we came to a place in a poplar grove where there was a break in the trees and underbrush. A water channel ran in front of it and there was a fine view of the mountains. So we sat down there to look and rest. At the pool Batul had found an unsmoked cigarette, and this we decided to put on a stone along with two matches for the pleasure of someone who might come along and, like us, want to pause there. Nasair, however, doubted that anyone would smoke it. "They will think that it is poisoned," he said. It reminded me of Marcellus, a Roman soldier who, writing about the Iranians in the third century, reported that they never ate fruit in places unknown to them, fearing poison or spells.

But in the end it was smoked, for just as we were about to go, a dark, wicked-looking fellow with a staff came marching along. At our invitation, he squatted down beside us and smoked the cigarette quite happily. We talked about the different springs in the mountains about which he seemed to know a great deal. One was for barren women, another was for those who had no appetite, and still another apparently was aphrodisiac, for he said that it made a man act like a goat. After he had gone, the herd boy, who was still with us, told us that the fellow was a "brave and famous thief."

Before reaching the Garden, we had still another encounter, this time with the local madman, whom I had heard about but had never seen. He was a tall, unsteady figure, ragged and soiled, lurching about in the lane as though he were drunk. He said something to me and, not understanding, I said, "What?"

"Oh, I wasn't talking to you," he said reprovingly. So we went on, but he followed us, calling out nonsense to the orchards we passed. "Where is the donkey? . . . Come, it's time for lunch. . . . What lusts are you up to there beneath the trees?" Then once again he addressed me.

"Has Your Honor been picnicking?"

"Yes," I said.

"Oh, I wasn't talking to you," he replied. "I was talking to someone else."

Nettled, I took the children's hands and we walked faster, trying to leave him behind us.

When we reached the gate of the Garden, he yelled at us.

"Look, look, this is backward." We turned and indeed there he was hopping backward down the lane.

"Don't let him in!" said Khanom, who was waiting for us at the gate. "He will want to stay, and then I shall have to take a stick and beat him to make him go out." Then she went off to the bakehouse and came back with bread, which she gave to Nasair to give him.

We went in then and, thirsty, drank some limeade under the trees and talked about the picnic.

Ra'is Ali's assistants have begun to harvest the dog rose. Mahmud is ten and Jafar, eight; they have shaven, jelly-bean-shaped heads, long-tailed indigo shirts, striped pajamas, and bare feet. Around their middles they each wear a thin red towel, gathered at the front to form a pouch to hold the blossoms. They work quietly and slowly and peer at each blossom before they pick it. What are they looking at or for? Simply the blossom itself, I suppose. They reach what they can from the ground. For higher up, they have a stool and stand on its rungs or sit cross-legged on its top. When they stand on the low rungs, Nasair and Batul tickle their feet. They don't complain but simply lift their feet as if flies had settled on them.

Wherever they are, they always carry with them a black kettle, two glasses, a paper of tea, and a handkerchief of lump sugar. More often than not, they are having tea instead of working, facing each other cross-legged and talking quietly like old men. When they see me, they bob their heads and call out some courtesy such as "We are your slaves." But as soon as my back is turned they laugh.

*

This morning, very early, returning from partridge shooting, I heard a harness jingling and, looking across a plowed field, I saw a cart come suddenly around the corner of a wall. The horse was black; the cart was two-wheeled and flat with a man standing on top of it, his knees bent to brace himself. In one hand he held the reins and in the other, a whip, flung out. The thing rattled past me at a terrible clip; as it did, the man called down a greeting to me and, smiling with a flash of teeth, snapped his whip at the sky.

Last night in the village I saw a crowd around the teahouse. Carpets hung down from the balcony and on the balcony itself there were several musicians. It reminded me that it was the birthday of the shah and that the people were celebrating with a stick dance.

I had a foreign friend with me and asked her if she wanted to see the dance. She did, so I stopped the Landrover and we went over to the crowd. Though we protested, they brought chairs for us and put them by the edge of the beaten ground before the teahouse, where the dances would take place. When we took our places, men with switches were cutting away at the legs of little boys in order to clear the space. This accomplished, the master of ceremonies told us that the first dance would be done by women since that would be more "delicate" for us — and he bowed toward my companion.

The women came out. One was little more than a child; the second, in her late teens; the third, an older woman. They were dressed, rather like tribal women, in full petticoats, and their headdresses had gold coins sewn into them. In each hand they held a long gauze scarf.

The dance was formal, slow, and repetitious. It consisted of a few steps forward, a few back, and turns — the head down, arms out, the scarfs flowing. It went on for some time. We watched the dancers. The crowd watched us. As the dance neared its end, the rhythm grew faster and we all began to clap the beat. When it was finished the crowd called out several tributes: one for the shah, one for the dancers, and one for "our dear guests." Then tea was brought.

Next the stick dancers came on — two men. One held in both hands, horizontally, a long thick stick. The other held a much thinner one vertically. For a time the two danced independently — a hopping kind of dance with turns. Suddenly the thick stick rushed the thin stick, driving him back into the shadows. Points are scored by the number of times they succeed in touching each other's legs or feet, but all the while they must continue to dance.

It's a dramatic thing to watch, especially in such a setting: the shadows and light thrown by the flares, dust clouds rising from the rush of the feet, the faces straining from the sidelines, the suspense while the dancers indolently turn, the spectators not knowing when they will strike. In certain ways it is so Iranian — that lazy, beguiling grace suddenly becoming a sharp thrust, and also that old urge of theirs to ornament everything, even combat, making it a dance.

When we left, they called out another tribute to us: "Long life to our guests."

We are at the peak of autumn. The orchard is a paisley of yellow, rust, and orange, and the mountains, as always in autumn, are blue till noon. The autumn thieves are

with us too, the jackals and foxes that slip in at night to
see what they can filch, for there are no grapes or melons
left in the open country. That strange autumn wind has
begun as well, making all of us so sleepy, even the dogs.
They say that it blows on until it reaches the grave of a
poet about twenty miles from us, and that there it ends,
and in fact it does.

It was such a fine evening that I wanted to be out in it,
and so I went down to cut dead stalks out of the lilac
bushes. Mamdali came and asked me to stop. The spar-
rows, he said, went there at dusk to nest and I was dis-
turbing them. "It has sin," he added. By now it was
growing dark, and I went back to the house and lit the
first fire of the season.

The Visit of the Jester

It was once — and to some extent still is — the custom of certain rich old Iranian families to keep among their house servants a jester, a person to clown for them and tell them stories and be the butt of their jokes. I knew such a family in Tehran, and they had a jester named Akbari who had been with them for many years and to whom they were much attached.

One summer Akbari came to stay with us. He had been ailing, and his master thought a few months in the country might do him good. He knew, too, that I liked Akbari and would enjoy having him as my guest.

Instead of arriving on the day specified in the telegram, he came a week later and at two in the morning. I woke up to hear an awful commotion from the dogs mixed with the shouts of Mamdali. Half-asleep, I wondered what calamity had struck us. Then the garden lights went on and I realized that we had a guest, not a thief. Getting up, I went to the door, and there was Akbari at the bottom of the steps, stooped and thin-shouldered in an old cloak and holding a battered valise.

"I am half-dead," he called up to me. I learned that it had been an eighteen-hour journey by bus and that he was *khomar*, the condition of an opium smoker whose opium has been withheld — in this case, by the long bus journey. When I reached the bottom of the steps, he greeted me in the old way, bending to kiss my hands, and then he began to whimper for a brazier and charcoal so that he might get started on his opium. While Mamdali went off to get these things, I took his valise and led him down to the summer sitting room.

Sitting down on the sofa, his thin old legs jutting like jackknife blades under the cloak, his arms crossed against his breast, he began to rock back and forth, crooning to the thing that nagged inside him. "Wait, you brat," he whispered. "Your pap is coming. Be quiet."

He had a curious face. It was like some primitive mask, triangular in shape, the knobs of the cheekbones supporting the cranium like brackets, a big fierce beak of a nose, the thin lavender lips of the opium addict. And like a mask, it was a dead, immobile face. Only the eyes had life: they were large and full and flashed out his moods — temper, pain, or gentleness.

With a last, "Be quiet!" to his craving, he put his hands together like a man in prayer and, bowing toward me, he began to sing out the greetings of the family, delivering these with much solemnness but at the same time lampooning each greeter as he went along. "Mahin, the saintly sister of the beloved master, she whose behind puts to shame the elephant's, remembers you in her prayers. . . . Our dear little Asghar, pure fresh bud of the family bough — who was recently caught with his tool in a goat — conveys to you. . . . Rostam Aqa, prince of quacks, tells me to tell you. . . ." And on he went, reflecting like a funhouse mirror each member of the family — as I had often seen him do, with the fool's impunity, even in their presence, and to their delight.

After a while I touched his knee and told him to rest, for I knew what pain he was in, but he continued, like the classic clown, buffooning in the teeth of his misery. It was like his life, about which I knew something from his master: a mother so ill tempered that at ten he had been forced out to half-starve as a travelling magician's apprentice; the small inheritance swallowed up by a gambling brother; the beautiful girl who had turned into a barren

shrew of a wife; the greengrocer shop which had burned
to the ground. It had been a life filled with misfortune,
and yet, mixed in with all of this, there were wonderful
tales, half-Rabelaisian, half-Till Eulenspiegel, of larks and
sprees and outrageous high jinks. It was as a dancing
cripple that he had gone through life.

Akbari stayed with us almost all the summer. From the
first day, he established his routine. In a summer of terrible heat, he kept to the sitting room, sleeping on and off,
until late afternoon. Then, with the beginning of coolness, his day began. First came a dip in the pool. He had
no bathing suit but used instead an all-purpose square of
black silk. At night he wore it babushka-style to keep off
nonexistent drafts, looking, as Mamdali said, like a witch
at a funeral. For the dip in the pool, he tied it around his
genitals into a kind of pouch. Attired in this makeshift
bikini, little more than a rib cage and long sticks of limbs,
he would step into the water with the graveness of an old
crane and stand there blinking at the shock of the cold.
Then, calling on God to temper the water, he would squat
shoulder deep, scissor his legs, and begin to paddle dog
fashion, holding his head well back so that his mustache,
which he dyed with shoeblack, would not get wet and run.
The dip ended with a sudden little duck dive, his bare old
mottled bottom pointed to the heavens.

The next item in his routine was the saying of the evening prayers. Mamdali would lay out the carpet by the
side of the pool, placing his prayer stone at one end of it.
Akbari, having dried himself and put on pajamas and a
rag of a shirt, would kneel down at the other end, change
the position of the stone several times, and then begin
the intonations and bowings. It was a pleasure to watch him
pray. This was no duty but rather something to be drawn
out and slowly enjoyed, like an evening walk.

Ending his prayers with a long, dying call on God's mercy, he would return firmly to this world and announce his evening's needs: the brazier, the opium pipe, his tea, the lamps — for by now it would be almost dark — and what he had in mind for supper.

The opium came first. Mamdali and Nasair would bring the heavy brazier and, swinging it down in front of him, wish him a pleasant evening. Then out of the old valise came his smoking accouterments: the pipe in its blue velvet case, the fine steel tongs embossed with brass, a cigarette holder made of mulberry wood, the little box of opium — all carefully laid out in front of him. There were also the tea things: teapot, glass and saucer, the kettle in a corner of the brazier. Finally, Mamdali would bring the lamps — tall brass candlesticks fitted with frosted globes — and put them to either side of him. He looked like an old idol there between his lamps, the articles of his rite set out before him.

It was a pleasure to watch him pray, and it was a pleasure to watch him smoke. Opium smoking has its form as much as archery or sitting a horse, and he was most accomplished in it. He would sit very straight, the long pipe slanting down from his mouth, his right arm working the tongs as a violinist works his bow, deftly playing the charcoal over the opium to make it sizzle and release its smoke; then in quick little gulps he would draw in the smoke to pour it out again in perfect funnels from each corner of his mouth.

When one portion of opium was finished, he would put the pipe down and break a cigarette in two, putting one half in the holder, and lighting it with a piece of charcoal. Next he would set about the preparation of his tea, scalding the glass and saucer with boiling water from the kettle, pouring the tea, spooning in sugar, tasting to see that it was the proper strength and sweetness, and finally filling the glass to the brim with more boiling water. He did all these things slowly and with care, handling each object — saucer, glass, and kettle — with gentleness, as if they were pieces in some rare collection.

It was during these intervals between opium portions that he often told us stories or did little tricks of sleight of hand, or sometimes, flapping about in his cloak, imitations of us or other people. Now and then he closed his eyes when we laughed, and it seemed to me with weariness. There was always that twist; he would never let anything go without showing its other side, the bad behind the good, the good behind the bad. One evening, in a fretting mood, he spat in the pool and said, "They say that somewhere in the world there is a town where, when an infant is born, the people weep and beat their breasts, but when a man dies they blow horns and rejoice. Now those are people who know what the world's about." While he was saying this, a white kitten of ours wandered into his lap. He was about to spit again when he noticed it. "Ha!" he said, and took the kitten up into his arms, fondling it, and then held it out at arm's length, cooing to it, the anger gone from his eyes. But then he made no claim to consistency, any more than he asked for it in life.

Like any showman, Akbari was at his best when he had an audience, and it happened that summer that we had a fair number of guests, among them Mr. Dadgah, my hunting companion, and other people out from the town in the evening to escape the heat. We would sit by the pool talking until I or someone else — sometimes Mr. Dadgah, for he liked the jester very much — would ask Akbari to give us a story or one of his shadow-plays. If we were adults, the performances were usually salacious. If children were present, he would tell some innocuous fable which, in asides to the adults, took on other meanings. There was, for example, the tale of the lovesick frog. At one point in the story, by some trick with his hand in the pool, he would produce a high spurt of water. To the children this was the frog on his way across the pool to visit his lady love. The adults, however, would learn that it was a young man on his wedding night.

Among the shadow-plays, a favorite was the one about a mullah — a Moslem cleric — and a barren woman. Akbari, moving his hands against a tablecloth held up by Mamdali, and blowing a shrill little whistle as accompaniment, would show us the poor woman beseeching the mullah for a charm to end her barrenness. The mullah wanted money; the woman was penniless. With that the figures froze on the screen, and Akbari would turn and tell us that the play could not proceed until the poor woman was provided with some funds. It didn't take long for his audience to get the point, and coins would be thrown onto his square of black silk. Once again the figures would come to life, the mullah bobbing back and forth, pontificating, and telling the woman that she must give him her perfect trust and that he would end her barrenness. Then, suddenly, the shadows on the cloth would start into violent movement and there would be heard a smack — the mullah planting a kiss. In that instant while the children laughed, their heads thrown back, the adults would see the mullah's great penis poking out.

Sometimes Akbari would tell a story meant only for the children. On one of his last nights at the Garden, several children sat cross-legged in a circle around him and begged him to tell a story. The dogs were there as well, forming an outer circle, their heads down on their paws, ears cocked as though they, too, were listening. His finger raised, like a wand enchanting them, he began some tale about a lazy turtle and a crafty fox. Some of the children were foreign and knew no Iranian, but it made little difference. It was enough for them to watch him contort his face to suggest the figures of his story and to listen to his voice imitating the fox's sharp bark, the turtle's grunting. One could almost follow the story in their faces — the widening eyes, the frowns, the lips bunching to form a whistle of surprise — or, when the story took some particularly absurd and delightful turn, one could see them smile at one another in their pleasure. When the story ended and they were released from his spell, their faces would fill with wonder and sadness.

And so our summer evenings passed, the program rarely varying: the dip, the prayers, the pipe, the tea, the stories and tricks, and finally dinner, which we took on a wide plank stretched across the pool, the water to either side of us. Throughout the stifling days I would look forward to those evenings. It was not only that it soothed me to watch the respect and gentleness which Akbari gave to all objects and acts but also that what he said filled some need in me which had seldom before been satisfied. For he passed on a mood, calming as the opium which calmed him, a mood which made the world seem right. With his talk, with his simple being, he blended things which for me had always jarred and had sometimes canceled each other out — the absurd and the sacred, grief and joy — putting them together into one whole.

So when the letter came from his master ordering his return — Mahin, the one whose behind outdid the elephant's, was ill and wanted him there to comfort her and to tell her stories — I was sorry, so sorry to see him go. But there was no way out. "I must go to the sow's bedside," he said.

It took some time, however, to get him on his way.

Khanom insisted on mending and washing his cloak, while Mamdali, who disapproved of the battered valise, had a new one made for him in town — one with special compartments for the pipe, the opium box, the prayer stone, the other things — and all this took several days. Finally, we had to decide upon and then gather together the presents from the farm to be carried by him for the family: walnuts and pomegranates, a bottle of rose water, some wild tulip bulbs.

The day came for his departure, and when he was ready — smelling of the DDT which he had mistaken in my dressing room for foreign cologne — we all got into the Landrover, even the dogs, and took him off to town. Tottering on the step of the bus, stooped in his cloak, he was as always: cracking jokes, his eyes a little wet with tears.

When we got back to the farm, I found that he had forgotten the square of black silk. We wrapped it in tissue paper, slowly and with respect, as he would have done, and then put it in the Bombay chest to keep.

Journal III

THIS GARDEN IS, after all, the world; there is a serpent in
it. And that serpent is Ra'is Ali. Though perhaps it
would be more accurate to call him a spider — that round
black head hunched down between his shoulders, the little
eyes, the quick and bandy legs.

I do not know if Machiavelli has been translated into
Iranian, but it would be superfluous to do so, for his subject is one in which the Iranians need no instruction. It
must have been several months ago that Ra'is Ali came to
me and said that a plague of wasps had descended and
was devouring all the bees of our area, including my own.
I told him to go to work with the DDT. A few weeks later
he reported that the DDT had not been effective and that
now there were fewer bees left than the fingers on his
hand. In the local way, I raised my eyes to heaven indicating that God's ways were not to be questioned.

Now it happened that a day or two later, Mamdali
passed through an unfrequented corner of the orchard
gone wild with old spent trees. And what should he come
upon there but two new empty clay hives. Mamdali was
also born knowing his Machiavelli, and so he went up to
the stable wall where we shelter our hives and made a
small, distinctive mark on the back of each.

A week later the treachery revealed itself. Mamdali
and I had been off on some errand. Returning, we were
met by Ra'is Ali, his long legs and arms folding and un-
folding, his face drawn down in mournfulness, his eyes
bright. The wasps, he told us, had devoured every last
one of the bees. We went to investigate. On the way, we

were met by Khanom, who sidled up to report that during our absence Ra'is Ali had left the garden with his donkey burdened down under a load of some kind concealed beneath a blanket.

The hives appeared to be in perfect order, resting as usual on their sawhorses, covered as usual by the old comforter. Only, as Ra'is Ali sorrowfully told us, they were quite empty. We then proceeded to check the back of the hives. Mamdali's special marks were missing, and we knew then that the full hives had been replaced with the duds from the corner of the orchard. Wrath fell and, with a volley of curses and threatened sticks and stones, the serpent was driven from the Garden.

But only temporarily. The man was born here and putting him out of the Garden for good is as unthinkable as uprooting the cypress. So he is back, but without his salary and, worse, without his title "Ra'is," which in his case means master gardener. He has been degraded to simple Ali.

Unlike me, Mamdali is shocked not so much by the thievery — and not at all by the method, which he considers admirably ingenious — as by Ali's ignorance of religious tradition. Everyone knows, he told me, that bees were particularly beloved by the Prophet and thus stolen bees will never, never give honey. I hope that he is right.

Last night we had our first snowfall. In melting it must have shorted a wire, for about two in the morning the house bell began to ring in Mamdali's quarters and would not stop. He thought that the thieves had come at last and that I was ringing for help. When he came into my room and found that this was not the case, he woke me anyway so that I might see the snow. And so we stood there for a little while by the opened window watching it fall. We knew that in the morning there would be much work for both of us, getting out the long poles and knocking the snow from the weaker branches and the wires. But for the moment it was most agreeable to watch the flurries and to see the blackness of the trees against the white. I knew, too, that if the snow lasted long enough, its water slowly drenching the ground, the summer would be very green.

Yesterday I took the old road back from Hassanabad, wanting to see that part of the country. I was perhaps halfway along when the radiator began to overheat. Looking around for trees or a village, somewhere to get water, I saw to my left, about a mile away, what appeared to be black blankets spread along the hills — a tribal encampment. There was no road to it, so I just drove across the desert.

I parked at the bottom of a draw that led up to the camp, a scattering of black goat-hair tents. Some men waited for me at the top. When I had gone a little way, several came down to greet me. "Welcome," they called out. After I explained my visit, we went up together. At the top I shook hands with the rest. They had, like so many tribesmen, that look which I have only seen before in Byzantine icons and in the faces of the Aran Islanders — a kind of stunned staring, like men caught dreaming of eternity. In the case of the icons, I do not know the reason for this look — perhaps the saints saw God — but with the tribesmen and the Aran Islanders, it may be that men who all their lives have before them

great unbroken sweeps of sky and land are left wide-eyed
and somehow dazed.

Their women were there too, on the far side of the
wood smoke, crouching at a loom — a long, narrow frame
set on pegs a few inches above the ground and warped in
strands of orange, green, raspberry, and blue. Two of
the women stood up to see me better. They wore, like all
tribal women, long, colored petticoats — six or seven of
them — of shot silk, satin, sequinned stuff; it struck me
then, as it had before, what comely concealments these
were, for surely with the miles and miles that tribal
women walk and climb they must have thighs like wres-
tlers and buttocks like dray horses. The petticoats, however, not only hid all this but also gave them, tall and
straight as they were, a swinging majesty. They wore, too,
the usual abbreviated veil, more a headdress really, of colored gauze tied into a kind of circlet around their heads
and falling down their backs. Gold coins on a looped
chain lay across their foreheads.

While someone went to get a skin of water for the radiator, the *kalantar* came out of his tent to greet me. A
kalantar is the chief of a subtribe. This *kalantar* was an old
man, stooped and sunken-cheeked, with worried, sad
eyes. These are hard days for the tribes, with their old
life breaking up, and so for their leaders there are perhaps too many problems.

He invited me to his tent and I went, knowing that to
just take the water and go was out of the question. His
tent, like the others, was shaped like a lean-to, a flap at the
front. Inside the place was wainscoted with *gelim,* the
kind of thing the women were weaving, striped stuff like
Joseph's coat. There were *gelims,* too, on the ground,
some bolsters, and in the center an open fire pit. The
mesh of the goat-hair cloth was open enough to let in a

blur of light but oily to keep out the rain, which now, lightly, had begun to fall. Down at the end there was a wattled wall with a few lambs and chickens on the other side of it.

They brought me a skewer of kabobed liver, sheep's milk, and bread — paper thin, salty, and crisp. The *kalantar*'s children, perhaps grandchildren, asked me for a corner of the bread to feed their birds. These were tiny creatures, long beaked and full breasted, each with a thread tied to its beak; in this way the children would play with them, the little birds hopping about, the children laughing. Sometimes, too, the children would bring from behind the wattle a chicken or a lamb to show me and then to play with.

The *kalantar* said that he had a question to ask me. Since my countrymen were rich, was it not possible for them to sit all day and think? I told him they did not. He was puzzled. Then he went on to say that he was certain that if he sat thinking for a year or two — it might take three — he would be able to conceive the construction of a radio. Having done so, he would simply go to town, buy wire and metal, and make it. He added that sometime, as a kind of experiment, he might do this. Then he picked up the thread of one of the little birds and, staring at the fire, began to play with it.

I had become sleepy, from the rain perhaps and the wood smoke. I told the *kalantar* that with his permission I would sleep, though outside, for now the rain had stopped and the air was very fresh. They picked up a length of goat-hair cloth and a *gelim* to put on top of it and found me a hollow near the camp. I asked them to wake me when the sun reached the beginning of its last quarter, for I wanted to be on my way before nightfall.

I woke up to the sound of the herds, the bonging of

their bells. For a little while I lay, eyes closed, listening. Then I opened them and saw that it was dusk. The herds were funneling in through the ravines and down over the sides of the hills. I got up and walked to the rim of the camp to make water. The plain stretched flat and dim to the far mountains — so far that they seemed like the last boundaries of the earth. I turned back to the camp, the tents in the darkening light like bat wings settled on the slopes, the herds in white smudges drifting toward them. The evening fires had been started; sparks were blowing in the smoke and I could see in outline the bending figures of the women. From behind the hills, which were black and craggy now, came the rising moon. I wanted to stay but I knew I couldn't.

The *kalantar* and some of the others came up to me. The food, they said, would soon be ready, and after that I could sleep again. I looked at their faces and at the fires and again I was tempted. But I had made certain promises. They did not say that I should break the promises, but only that I should put them off for another day. I started walking to the Landrover. They came along with me, looking puzzled and hurt. "Why?" the *kalantar* asked. "After all there is time — time," and he motioned toward the plain, the mountains, and the sky.

The Passion Play

O NE SPRING I took the Arab mare to a village across the mountains to have her bred. On the way back an axle broke. When I got out to see what had happened, I heard the braying of *shaypurs* from the hills behind me. A *shaypur* is a six-foot wooden horn with a brass flare at its end, the kind of thing played from draped balconies in the Middle Ages.

After checking the axle, I looked around to see where the music came from, thinking there might be some help from the players. I was in an amphitheater of hills still green from the spring rains, and it was in a long draw between two of these that I saw the horsemen and their glinting horns. It puzzled me. Why should men be cantering up and down a mountain draw blaring *shaypurs*? I took out my field glasses, and with these I could see that the men carried black banners. Then I understood.

The Iranians observe two calendars: a civil calendar, which is solar, and a religious lunar one. The religious year, like the civil one, has its months, and we were then in Moharram, a month of mourning. The mourning commemorates the martyrdom of Hussain, grandson of the Prophet, on the plain at Karbala in Iraq in 680. Because Hussain was one of the first protagonists of the predominantly Iranian sect of Shiah Islam, his killing has come, in the common mind, to symbolize the oppression from which the Iranians have suffered so often. In this month of Moharram there are two days of particularly deep mourning: Tassu'a, the day of Hussain's agony, and Ashura, the day of his death. When I saw the black banners carried by the horsemen, I remembered that it was the day of Tassu'a.

The horsemen were too far away to hear me call, especially above the braying of the dirge, and so I decided to signal them with my shirt. I was just about to do this when a man on a black horse came down the road. He was wearing the full black trousers of the peasants of that area and a black satin shirt — a rather somber figure there on his black horse, except that with his free hand he was twirling a rose and in his face there was considerably less piety than mischief. He cocked an eyebrow at me and then, putting the rose between his teeth, he slipped off the horse and swaggered over to the Landrover.

"I am Gholam Ali, your servant," he said. "What is this misfortune that has befallen you?"

I told him what had happened. He immediately proposed a solution. A bus would be leaving his village the next morning and all I had to do was give the driver money for a new axle, which would then be brought back on the driver's return. He, Gholam Ali, "an accomplished mechanic," would replace the broken axle with the new one. I had had dealings with these accomplished mechanics before and, further, I knew that whether the bus in fact departed in the morning depended on "God's will" — that is to say, on the driver's whim. However, there being nothing else to do, I agreed. Where I was to stay until the axle was replaced was settled also. I would, of course, Gholam Ali said, be the guest of his master. I knew enough about country ways to know that the offer was sincere and also that I, as a foreigner, would be a welcome curiosity and diversion for whoever his master might be.

These matters settled, we took the mare from the trailer and together trotted down the road, out of the little amphitheater of hills, with its horsemen and blaring horns, and on to the long poplar alley that led to the village.

We hadn't gone far before Gholam Ali turned to me and said, "In fact your bad fortune is your good fortune."

"And how is that?" I asked.

"Because tonight you will be our guest at *ta'ziyeh*."

A *ta'ziyeh* is a passion play. There are many of these plays and most of them portray some aspect of Hussain's agony on the plains at Karbala. I had never seen a *ta'ziyeh* and, further, I was aware that foreigners are not welcome at them. I mentioned this to Gholam Ali.

"Nonsense," he answered. "And anyway, I am the lion of this village and I invite you."

The lion, I knew, plays a part in some of the scenes. At various times he attempts to come to the aid of Hussain, and also, when Hussain's severed head is being carried to the caliph, a lion by the roadside bows low before it.

Gholam Ali, it turned out, was the hereditary lion of the village, his ancestors having always played the part. Turning grandly in his saddle, he told me that he had a new costume of gazelle skins.

"I am a splendid sight," he said.

By now we had reached the village square, where a great commotion was taking place. *Dastehs* from different quarters of the village were coming in and merging there. A *dasteh* is a religious brotherhood of the men of a neighborhood. In the old days they carried on their backs huge mourning floats, but now their principal activity is to walk in processions and flagellate themselves. It was these *dastehs* — there were three of them — which were coming out of the lanes into the dusty square with its mud walls draped in black.

At the head of each *dasteh* men carried enormous velvet umbrellas of different colors — salmon, green, and red — brilliant against the brown-black square. Behind came more men holding long poles from which hung black velvet banners embroidered with the monogram of the martyr. Next came one man, alone, who held the great standard supported in a socket strapped to his waist. The standard consisted of five plume-shaped plaques of silver rising from a silver crossbar that streamed with colored scarfs. The silver plumes represent the five members of the holy family: Mohammed; Fatima, his daughter; Ali, his cousin and son-in-law; and Ali's sons, Hussain and Hassan.

Following the standard came the body of the *dasteh,* two or three hundred men in black trousers and shirts. In the first half of the procession were the flagellants. Each man held a wooden rod with a tassel of chains attached to it. Walking with a long, jerking stride, they flung the chains down over one shoulder, then over the other, chanting as they scourged themselves, "Yah Hussain." Separating them from the second half of the procession, a man walked banging cymbals to give their scourging its rhythm. Behind him came men who, to the rhythm of the cymbal, struck their breasts with the flat of their hands. It was a strange symphony: the tinkling chains, the clanging cymbal, the deep, hollow booming of the struck chests, the keening chant. There was another sound too, but from the people who milled in the square: it was their low sobbing.

"With your permission," said Gholam Ali, taking his chains out of his saddlebag, "I will go and join them for a moment."

"Be careful," I said. "Don't wound yourself." He winked at me.

"Under this black shirt I wear two sweaters." Then he strode off to take his place in the procession, swinging the chains down on his back with impressive force.

I sat the horse there by the side of the square, taking in

the scene. The leaders of the three *dastehs* were now shaking hands. Little boys skittered across the square. Someone ran up to the cymbal player with a message: nails were wanted from his shop. A woman, stooped with what appeared to be the beginnings of her labor, walked between two other women out of the square. Faintly from the distance came the sound of the horns, and looking up I saw the tiny figures of the horsemen winding down the hills toward the village.

By now Gholam Ali was back.

"Come," he said. "We'll go to my master's house, where you may bathe and rest." And so we started out, across the square, down a lane into fields and orchards. My host, I found out, was to be the bailiff of the village.

Gholam Ali left me at the bailiff's door while he went in to inform his master of my coming. In a few moments the door opened and an old man in a black sugar-loaf hat and carrying black prayer beads stepped out, took my hand, and asked me to come in. It was the bailiff. I apologized for troubling him. He replied that my coming had made his house a garden.

We passed through a courtyard — potted geraniums, canaries in a cage, a pool — and into a small room at the end, which held nothing but a carpet and some bolsters. A servant brought tea and a plate of jasmine blossoms to scent the room.

The bailiff and I exchanged courtesies for a while and then moved on to who I was and whom we might know in common. It developed that the bailiff knew my grain merchant friend, Mr. Bazargan, and also in years past had known Salar Jang.

"May God rest his soul," the bailiff said of the latter. "He was extravagant in his pleasures, but he was a kindly man."

I could imagine, looking at the bailiff, that he did not much approve of extravagant pleasures. He had a prim old face, the slightly haughty look of a man forever concerned with the proper. But it was a tired face, too, which redeemed it a little. Certainly his job was a hard one, mediating between the landlord and the villagers. The thin, long-nailed hand that held the prayer beads trembled with palsy.

To reassure myself, I told him that Gholam Ali had invited me to the passion play and asked if my presence would be an intrusion.

"That thief," he said, referring to Gholam Ali. "Yes, of course, you are most welcome at the *ta'ziyeh*. I shall escort you there myself. But that Gholam Ali! Beware. The name Gholam Ali, as you must surely know, means the slave of Ali, but indeed sometimes I think he is the slave of Satan. With my own money I have sent him three times to the Shrine of Imam Reza to repent, but it has done no good. Beware that he doesn't steal your very shoelaces while he stands there beguiling you with his talk."

"But why do you keep him?" I asked. The old man raised the palsied hand to his eyes.

"Only God knows. I shall be consigned to the hell of fools." He shifted around on his haunches, as if seeking an answer. "Every time I try to put him out, he has some excuse. His family has worked for mine since God made the world — he says. His mother has gone blind. He needs money to buy a taxi and so become independent. Lies, lies, lies. He uses his money to do low things in the town, to buy those tight foreign trousers and strut about here in the village, a shame, a disgrace. Why, the fool even wears two wrist watches. Can you imagine such a showoff?"

Through this whole irascible recital I had sensed an undertone of something else, not sorrow exactly, nor bitterness, perhaps some mixture of the two. It was some time later, talking with Mr. Bazargan, that I learned that Gholam Ali was the bailiff's bastard.

Finally, the old man asked me if I would like to bathe and rest. He had a towel brought for me to wrap around myself when I went into the pool and told me that the room would be mine to rest in afterward. He left me with a pitcher of water and a fly swatter and said that we would start for the *ta'ziyeh* at seven that evening.

After bathing I slept. Once I woke up with the sense that someone was in the room. Through half-closed eyes, I saw Gholam Ali standing in the doorway, staring at my valise. I opened my eyes and looked squarely at him.

"It's a pity," he said. "Surely you have whiskey with you. There is a fine spring in the mountains and I have a drum which I play very well. We could go there. The problem — it's a pity — is that you have come in this mourning time. Still, perhaps, after the *ta'ziyeh* is over —," he winked and then he went away.

At six the bailiff had a light supper sent in to me and also a pair of black trousers and a black shirt to wear to the *ta'ziyeh*. A little later he came himself and said that it was time to go.

Outside waited a group of "white beards," the important elders of the village, grave old men with dignified, gaunt faces who wore, like the bailiff, the black, full-legged trousers of the place, black shirts, and black sugar-loaf hats. They were introduced to me and then we started out across the fields, the bailiff and I ahead, the old men — two by two — following us. We walked in a slow, measured way, not talking, and I felt more strongly than ever before a sense of procession, of stateliness, though it was only a field of spring wheat which we crossed.

From the fields we passed into the poplar alley and then down into the narrow clay-walled lanes of the village. We stopped at a place where three lanes met, a kite-shaped open space that had been draped with black cloths and filled with lights. In the center stood Hussain's catafalque. It was an enormous, hooded affair of black cloth stretched on a wooden framework, and mirrors covered the whole front of it. A few yards away a fire burned on top of a squat column, and there were pressure lamps hanging from wires strung from the walls, the lamps moving a little in the light wind of the evening. We stopped here, and in the ricocheting reflections of the mirrors, as piercing as strobe lights, the old men struck their breasts and hoarsely called out Hussain's name.

Then we proceeded across the open space and there, around the corner, we came to the archway of the *hussainiyeh* — as the place for a passion play is called — and found an usher waiting to escort us in. The scene was not what I had expected. I knew that it would be crowded, but I had thought the mood would be somber, not festive. This was like a market square on fair day: knots of people talking and laughing, others at a distance from each other calling and waving, women bouncing babies, boys tussling, tea carriers loping through the crowd with their trays high above their heads — a noisy, confused, happy gathering.

The site where all this was taking place was a courtyard of about seventy-five feet square, surrounded on all sides by brick walls. In each wall there were two tiers of five arched niches, each niche commodious enough to accommodate about twenty people. One wall higher than the others extended up into a third tier of arches in the form of a triptych. From the highest of the triptych arches flew a green flag, the only color in the structure, which was as bleached as bone in the moonlight.

The usher led us through the crowd to a niche which had been reserved for us. Here they had put — out of consideration, I suspected, for the foreign guest, for other people sat in the niches in the usual tailor fashion — a crude, local copy of a French settee. The old men stood for a moment bowing to friends in the crowd below, and then we all sat down and tea was brought.

Now I could see in detail where I was and what was going on. All the niches of the second tier were occupied by women, while those in the first tier contained a packed collection of everybody: families, old men, and children. People had also taken their places on blankets and carpets spread around the periphery of the court. The court itself, which I realized now was the stage, was filled with people, standing and chatting, and at one side there was a raised, railed platform, which I learned was "off-stage" for the actors despite the fact that it was in plain view of everybody.

Again, I was struck by how festive the people's mood was. Though I knew very well the Iranians' equal capacity for joy and grief, still this mixing of them seemed to my Western mind incongruous.

All kinds of high jinks were going on. In the niche next to us a bunch of guffawing boys were pouring water down on a group of ladies gathered on a carpet at the edge of the court. At one point one of the boys saw a woman who might have been his grandmother, and perhaps was — a well set up old Wife of Bath marching across the court — and called out to her. She stopped and called back to him, and then fishing down under her veils she brought out a handful of sweets, which she wrapped in a big colored handkerchief and threw to him. He missed, another of the boys catching the sweets, and she stood there laughing, clapping her belly.

By now about an hour had passed. The court still milled with people, no sign of any play except for a man — the director, I was told — who stood on the raised platform conferring with several other men. Then, with no announcement of any kind, a band of little boys entered the far side of the court carrying the black banners. They were, as the Iranians describe floundering clumsiness, "broken-armed and broken-legged," falling all over themselves, stumbling and veering, apparently with no idea of what they were supposed to do. Their entry was not, as it had seemed to me it would be, a sign for the audience to leave the stage. Audience and procession were all muddled together. The muddle became even greater when there next appeared two lines of flagellants led by six tall young sayyids — descendants of the Prophet — dressed in black satin shirts, black trousers, and green cummerbunds, green being the color of the Prophet's house. They were more figures from ballet than processionists. Moving forward in a long, gliding step, they would turn and bow to each other like courtiers in some elaborate presentation, then snap straight, their chains flaring like little fountains above their heads, and finally arch back and fling the chains down in unison across their shoulders, their faces — caught for the moment in the light — white, staring, and ecstatic. Gradually the hoarse shout which came with each downstroke of the chains submerged the murmur of the crowd. Suddenly there came into all of this a long, splitting trumpet blast. It was as if a curtain had parted to begin the play.

Three caparisoned horses with green head plumes were led into the court and held there by grooms. Next came

the trumpeter followed by ten drummers. The drums
were big bass affairs, beaten on one side with a heavy,
padded stick, on the other with a slender, ridged one, so
that two sounds issued from the drums: the deep bass
booming and a sharp ra-ta-tat staccato. Now and then the
drumming was pierced by a trumpet blast.

While this overture continued, the drummers moving
over into a corner of the court, the actors began to
wander in and mix with the audience, a large number of
whom still lingered on the stage. One of the actors I
recognized as Shemr, a figure who appears in many of the
passion plays. He was the Arab general sent by the caliph
to war against Hussain, and so is the villain of the piece.
Tonight Shemr was a little old man with white chop
whiskers, dressed in red robes and wearing a spiked hel-
met. The bailiff, who must have been in his late seventies, told me that as a child he had seen this same man
playing the part of Shemr, which meant that the man
must now be in his nineties. It did not surprise me; in the
villages around the farm I had often come on men who
were very old.

The old man, for all his years, seemed extraordinarily
vigorous, striding about the stage, making fierce practice
lunges with his sword. But when one of the green-
plumed horses was brought for him to mount, three
young men came forward and carefully lifted him up
onto the horse, holding him for a moment until he got his
balance. Once he was firmly seated in the saddle, a little
applause broke out from the crowd to which he gravely
bowed in acknowledgement. Then holding the reins
high, he began to trot smartly around the stage, calling
out in his high old man's voice — the drums rumbling an
accompaniment — a résumé of the play. We were to see
the story of the three-day thirst of Hussain on the deserts

of Karbala and of how the perfidious caliph's forces attempt to prevent him from bringing water to his family and men. It seemed odd to me that the villain should give this résumé until I remembered that the old man was being honored for his age.

By now the stage had been cleared somewhat of people, and men with willow whips had appeared, flicking at the legs of boys to get them back. More actors, too, were strolling in, stopping to shake hands and chat with people in the audience. Among them was Zainab, the wife of Hussain, played by a man, as were all the female parts. He moved in his skirts with the long stride of a ploughman and, through a hole in his face veil, smoked a cigarette in a long holder — a simple solution which, when he arrived on the stage, apparently struck no one as funny. More and more I began to realize that the conventions of Ibsen and Shaw had not touched *ta'ziyeh*.

Without our being quite aware of it, the play had started, for now Hussain himself had appeared and was pacing the center of the stage, his arms thrown out in the gestures of lamentation. Dressed in a brown camel's-hair cloak, a grey soutane, and a black circlet turban, he was a commanding figure — an old man, but tall and straight, shoulders back, his head riding in perfect poise and with a certain hauteur, his face as clear and finely formed as the face of a youth. Raising his arms like a dancer and swaying slightly, he began to sing in a thin but delicate tenor a kind of aria. It was difficult for me to follow: ". . . my people thirst. . . . they wither like grain in drought. . . . O God, grant us the water of thy mercy. . . ." the voice called on, ending at last in a long vibrato of grief. There was a pause, and then the voice of another player, the brother Hassan, began in consolation to answer him.

For a time the players continued to sing the arias to one

another, setting the situation of the play. I could only catch the general outlines. Hussain, his wife and children, his brother Hassan, and their men were camped at a place in the desert where there was no water. A half-day's ride away was the river Euphrates, but it was guarded by the caliph's forces. The director had left "off-stage" and was now mixing with the players down in the court. Sometimes he would give a push to a player who, chatting with someone in the audience, had forgotten that he was "on." And now and then the director would pass slips to the players — their lines, which they would glance at as they performed their parts.

So the play moved on informally, the audience quite as casual as the players. The stage was now entirely cleared, but occasionally someone from the audience would cross it on an errand, passing unconcerned through the players and their action. One of these was an old man carrying a pan of burning sticks with which to warm his niche, for the night was growing cold. The smoke from the sticks billowed up into the players' faces, and the play stopped while they coughed and blew their noses. Gholam Ali also appeared now, ostentatiously crossing the stage, draped in his gazelle skins and carrying a little hand drum. He sat down at the far side of the stage, opposite us, and waved. The bailiff moaned.

With a roll of the drums the play went into its second act, for the drums were used to indicate the breaks in action and were, in effect, the curtains of the acts. Hussain left his family and went off to storm the caliph's camp. This was represented by Hussain mounting a horse and galloping several times around the stage. Then, reaching his destination, he dismounted to find himself confronted by Shemr, the caliph's general. The two old men began a long swordplay, Shemr prancing about with great alacrity,

Hussain moving his sword with stateliness as though it were a baton and he was conducting a slow movement. The swordplay was obviously a favorite with the audience, only a few of whom were now talking among themselves. It was finally, however, disrupted by the lion, who suddenly made his appearance, cavorting between the combatants and getting in their way.

"The fool," mumbled the bailiff. "This play does not call for the appearance of the lion, but he will insist on imposing himself, wanting, I suppose, to show off those new skins of his — always wanting to show off, new skins or foreign pants." Meanwhile the director was leading Gholam Ali off the stage, the latter making deep bows to the audience.

Once again the drums rolled, and we were back at Hussain's camp. It was not entirely clear to me what had happened to Hussain himself, but at the camp a massacre had apparently taken place, a section of the caliph's forces, I gathered, having struck from the rear. Zainab, with her two children and a baby doll infant in her arms, strode up and down the stage, putting dust on her head and wailing. A bloodied sheet appeared, and the simulated stumps of two hands were held up and then thrown onto the pile of properties at the side of the stage. For a moment Zainab stopped in her wailing and the thin, pleading voices of the children rose into the night, cutting the heart; the old, hideous, inexplicable fact, the suffering of children. Then there began to mix with their cries another sound which for an instant, though knowing I must be wrong, I took for the cooing of doves, a kind of crooning. Looking around, I realized that it was the people, everyone — the bailiff, the rowdy boys, the lion — all softly weeping, the women bunching their veils to their faces, the men sobbing into the sleeves of their coats. The moon, now immediately above the court, was like the awful, pitiless eye of a malevolent universe staring down at us, and in its cold and hurting light the players and the people submitted to their grief.

Suddenly, as if to stop the grief, to break the blackness before it went too far — and that indeed may have been the intention — Hussain, who had now appeared, stepped out of his role for a few moments and became what he was in ordinary life, the village butcher. Standing in the center of the stage, he addressed the people, thanking them for coming to the *ta'ziyeh* from "near and far," the "far" being the players' gesture of welcome to me. He then went on to speak of the sick — to say that though their bodies were absent, their hearts were among us — and to offer prayers for them. As he spoke, old Shemr sat slumped on his horse, shivering. Indeed, the night had turned very cold and the ushers had brought us bowls of hot, sugared milk to drink and camel's-hair cloaks to put around our shoulders.

The oration finished, the play went on, depicting Hussain's horror at finding his men massacred and his brother, wife, and children dying of thirst. Meanwhile, the ushers were carrying envelopes from members of the audience to the various players. The envelopes contained messages of gratitude for their performance and sometimes money. Hussain blew into one to check how much money it contained and then tucked it into his soutane and went on with his lines. Now and then someone from the audience with a child in arms would walk into the middle of the performance and, approaching Hussain, hold out the child to receive his kiss.

With no announcement the play abruptly stopped even though, as the bailiff told me, it wasn't finished. It had been decided that it was too cold to go on, but it did not greatly matter, for its ending was known to everyone. The actors wandered over to the edge of the stage or up onto the railed platform, their places taken by a group of men who led in five sheep to be sacrificed. Straddling the sheep, they drove their knives in to the blare of trumpets, blood pooling in the dust of the court. Then they hoisted the sheep onto their shoulders and took them away to distribute to the poor while other men with shovels came and spread dirt over the blood. Now the ushers began to pass through the crowd, each usher carrying a small tin basin of water into which everyone put a little money. When this was finished, all the men in the place stood up and began in unison to strike their breasts while the women in the niches, their veiled heads in a moving frieze against the brick, rocked forward and began their keen. These sounds, the struck chests of the men and the keening of the women, blended, and it was as if great wings beat above us, beating down heavier and heavier on the whimpering, helpless cries, finally engulfing them. Then all was over. People jumped from the niches, others gathered up their carpets, and in a great press and babble of talk we were carried to the exits.

Outside there was the same happy, casual confusion we had seen on first entering the *hussainiyeh*. Girls darted down the lanes, their veils flying, motorcycles roared by, and a group of boys from a disbanded *dasteh* flicked their chains at one another like boys at home snapping towels in a shower room. The bailiff, however, and the other old men proceeded as sedately as ever, though chatting a little about the play, comparing it with former years, passing digs and compliments on the players.

We hadn't gone far before I felt a hand under my elbow. It was Gholam Ali, still draped in his skins.

"Come," he whispered. "Leave the old sticks. Get your

whiskey. I have the drum. We'll go to the spring and build a fire."

"On a night like this!" I said. "It would not be proper."

"Forget it," he said. "Come," he raised his hand to wipe at the tears which still smeared his face. "Come," he smiled. "Our passion is over."

As I had expected, it took several days to get away from the village because of the bailiff's hospitality and Gholam Ali's slowness in arranging for the axle. But finally it came and I was able to return to the farm. That winter the mare gave us a fine stud foal. And he was always for me a kind of remembrance of the village and the passion play, for he too was a gleaming black.

Journal IV

Firm instructions have been given to Ali's young assistants that they are not to strip the Garden of the wild narcissi — which they take to the town to sell — but to leave me at least a few. This morning in the orchard, fixing a prop for a heavy limb, I saw Nasair at a distance, a stick raised in his hand, rushing the two of them who were up to their old tricks behind some bushes.

"Dog's balls!" he yelled at them. "You know it has been forbidden."

"May he eat farts!" they called back to him, meaning me, not knowing that I was anywhere about. Nasair was not to be outdone.

"I fart in the beard of your grandfather!" he said, shaking his stick.

Anticipating a tussle, I coughed loudly. There was a thrashing sound, the assistants making off. Nasair came up to me.

"They are incorrigible," he said disgustedly and spat. I knew that he himself was not beyond selling some narcissi now and then. However, I am regularly paid off, so what can I do. Every morning in the narcissus season he brings me one as soon as I get up.

"Dog's balls," he said again in great indignation, and then went off with narrowed eyes to see what new tricks the assistants were up to, and perhaps this time to join them.

*

Such excitement! It seems the most important event to have happened in months, and in a way I suppose it is. The first kid of the season has been born.

The children came running up to get me, tugging at my hands, pulling me to the end of the orchard, their eyes wild, hardly able to talk in their excitement. The goat lay under a tree, a pool of blood and mucus at her hindquarters. Khanom was holding the kid to the mother's mouth so that she could lick it clean and warm it, for it was still wet with mucus and shivering. How enormously pleased we all seemed to be, standing there looking at the goat and kid — this little instance of the world turning in its proper course.

I have never seen the children so ecstatic. Perhaps it seemed to them that a miracle had taken place; then, too, this was something little like themselves, a companion almost, and one to whom an extraordinary thing had happened. Khanom, in her own way, appeared to identify as well. After all, here was a female like herself doing what only females can do. In a curious way her manner made Mamdali and me feel dismissed, relegated. Once when Mamdali stepped forward to shift the position of the goat, she gave him a look and he drew back. He had to content himself with saying that this kid, having dewlaps, would be called a sayyid, a descendant of the Prophet, in his village. He didn't seem to know the reason for this nor to consider it of much importance. I then asked him why the kid had dewlaps, what purpose they served.

"Oh, they are pretty," he said. "Why do women wear earrings?"

The children are still in high excitement and spend all their time with the goat and kid. Today we found that Nasair had fallen asleep with them, his head on the goat's flank. He tells me that he is going to give grass to the goat often during the day so that she will soon bear another kid.

I took a long walk this afternoon, up into the swells of the lower mountain slopes, my eyes riding the scene with the same sense of swinging ease that the body feels on a sled or skis following the contours of the earth. It all seemed so deserted, and yet I hadn't gone far before I heard a call. It came from two shepherd boys sitting on a slope a distance from me.

"Hello," they called down. "Are you sad? Why do you walk alone without a friend?"

A bit farther on, I came on an old man and a boy sitting by a water channel making tea. They invited me to join them. The old man's face was burned dark by the sun, and he had strong white hair and thick eyebrows which turned up at the ends. There were deep lines in the face but no wrinkles. I've often noticed this in peasant faces. Ours tend to crinkle up, cave in, but with them the skin remains firm and full of tone, and what lines there are, are deep and well defined as though a sculptor had put them in.

They had a skin of liquid yogurt with them and big flat rounds of bread wrapped in a dirty cloth. They emptied the yogurt into a tin basin and we each took our turn with the ladle. It was delicious, winey stuff and thick with mountain herbs. Then they untied the bread and rinsed out the tea glasses in the water channel.

We talked peasant talk: the crops, the weather, the rumor that a dragon had been seen at the holy tree, its coils wrapped around the trunk — and what did that portend? Then the boy asked me if I dyed my hair. I answered that I did not, not knowing whether he would believe me, for he had probably never seen a blond before. Next the old man asked if I was in the circus. Until a few days ago there was a small circus in the town. I suppose he had heard about it and it seemed to him the most likely explanation for my presence — this blond, blue-eyed foreigner up here in his hills.

After another glass of tea, I bade them goodbye. Like the shepherd boys, they did not approve of my walking alone, and so to keep me company they came along part of the way.

The dogs have been poisoned. It was on Tuesday, I believe, that, wanting to go for a walk, I called Wolf to come. He ignored me, lying there by the reservoir, and I went over to punish him for his disobedience. Then I saw that something was wrong. He was panting too much and his hindquarters were switched around in a funny way. I brought him water, which he drank but brought up again with black bile. Mamdali and I lifted him to take him to the shade. He was dead when we put him down again.

We went then to find Jock and Tobey. Their whimpering led us to them. They were stretched out flat by the channel that circles the *bonigah*, their noses in the water, trying to drink. I fixed a mustard emetic, but we couldn't get them to take it. Finally, they dragged themselves to a black hole under the foundation of the stables. They stayed there for three days, and we brought milk and water for them. Now they seem all right though still not quite their frisky selves. We think that Wolf, the much bigger dog, hogged most of the poison for himself, the others getting too little to kill them.

It could have been thieves but I doubt that. The thieves, I believe, have decided that it would be bad form to rob me. After all, I am a stranger and thus a kind of guest. It would be very Iranian of them to feel that I should be left alone.

But what has happened, or may have happened, is Iranian as well — revenge. Both Mamdali and I think it is the work of Ali in revenge for my having fired him. That I did so legitimately doesn't matter. I have hurt him and so he will hurt me back. Though I know that for most Iranians revenge is entirely respectable — in fact, one of the pleasures of life, like love and food — it still angers me, at least this instance of it does. And I would take action against him if I were certain that he was the poisoner, but I am not, for there is another possibility and it is very Iranian too. Someone — perhaps someone I hardly know — is envious of me for some reason and has decided to vent his feeling. Envy, it seems to me, is one of the national afflictions eating, like lye, at all of them. What a curious ingredient, this malice, to find alongside their compassion, and yet both, it seems to me, are in high proportion in many Iranians.

Jock and Tobey have begun to dig at Wolf's grave — because they miss him or because they want to eat him, I do not know — and we have had to cover the grave with brambles to keep them away from it.

The Winter Village

O<small>NE WINTER DAWN</small> Mamdali woke me to tell me that my friend Jahan Shah was waiting in the library. Dazed and wondering what the man could want at such an hour, I got up and went out to him.

He was standing with his back to the fire, legs spread, his sheepskin coat hiked up behind to keep it from the flame, and on his head a fleece stocking cap. It was perhaps the cap, and the way, helmet-like, it framed his face, that made him look that morning like one of the old Iranian folk warriors; he had a big head, the nose a little hooked, the eyes as black and full and filled with light as the eyes of a gentle animal.

Jahan Shah owned a village some fifty miles west of the farm, not far, in fact, from the village where I had seen the passion play. For the most part, however, he lived in town, for he enjoyed drinking, gambling, the companionship of many friends, and he was always after women — activities to which the town gave greater scope than the village. Among the townspeople he was known as a *luti*. There is, in this context, no equivalent to the word in English, but roughly it means a man who, above all things, values pleasure and faithfulness to friends.

As I have said, Jahan Shah and I were friends. We were not, however, friends in the way Mr. Dadgah, Mr. Bazargan, and others were, for we had very little in common. We simply liked each other, liking perhaps what the other had, the old attraction of opposites. Once I found him running his finger down the spines of my books, and sometimes he would ask with a shy deference hardly characteristic of him what studies I was up to. I, on the other hand, envied him for what seemed to me to be the largeness of his spirit, something robust and welcoming about him in his dealings with life.

When I came up to him at the fire, he put his arm around my shoulder and began to rock me back and forth, chiding me for not having been up with the dawn. Then, ordering Mamdali to bring him brandy, he sat down and explained his visit. The ewes were lambing early at his village and for this reason, plus some other business, he was going there. Would I like to come along?

"You are too much alone," he said, leaning forward, snapping his fingers between his legs, frowning at me. "It is not good for your mind. Only the mad, and sometimes the very holy, should be alone." He tossed the brandy down and turned to Mamdali. "Pack his things," he said.

The ride to the village was a bleak and wintry one: the sky hung low with soiled grey bags of clouds; the desert was dead and leaden as a sullen sea; and, worst of all, an evil wind flapped and whirled like a poltergeist, slapping us with the bitter cold. The village, a rather new one, looked even more depressing than the landscape — a grid of raw clay cubes set in the middle of a large and empty plain. Lights burned dimly here and there. Brown slush lay everywhere. It could not have been less inviting, and I thought of the Alpine villages of Europe with their golden windows beneath snow gables, their promise of pine, reflecting brass, and firelight. Here, I felt, one would crouch in shadows, pummeled by the poltergeist.

Jahan Shah's house lay on the outskirts of the place. In low gear we drove down the muddy potholed lane and stopped at a studded door. A short tunnel led to a farmyard — a pool of mud, manure, and straw — and from this another tunnel into a second courtyard, the living quarters. At the far end there were wide French windows topped by a fan of colored glass.

"They have the *korsi* ready," said Jahan Shah, motioning toward the room behind the windows, "and we shall snuggle in and have some brandy with our tea."

A *korsi* consists of several things. First is a clay pot of charcoal, the charcoal swung in a wire basket beforehand to rid it of its smoke and fumes. The pot is then put under a low table at the center of a small, mattressed room, and over the table and all of the room is spread a comforter. There are bolsters along the walls to sit against, the rest of the body under the comforter, the table there for work or food. These heated nests are used in all the colder parts of Iran and are an agreeable and cheap way of keeping warm in winter.

At the entrance to the room, we took off our shoes and pants, put on pajamas, and slipped in under the comforter. Our bodies, stiff and cold from the journey, sank gratefully into the enfolding warmth.

"Ah," moaned Jahan Shah as he stretched and turned his long body, luxuriating in the comfort and, at the same time, taking in deep breaths of the snow-cold air which came through the open doors. "What pleasure the body gives." Then he called for the servant to bring the tea and brandy.

Lulled by the warmth and the drink, our heads began to nod and we were almost asleep when a tapping at the window roused us. It was Jahan Shah's shepherd come to report on the sheep. He stood in the courtyard, talking to us through the open doors.

"How is your stomach?" Jahan Shah yelled at him.

"It still grinds like a mill, Your Honor," the man replied, and I looked at his face, stiff and thin, the eyes too bright. They went on to talk about the sheep. A dozen or so had lambed, more were due that night. Jahan Shah fished a bill out of his shirt pocket and gave it to the shepherd.

"Buy yourself medicine, but mind you keep your eye on the lambing or I'll have you whipped." The shepherd half knelt and then got up and went away.

I saw now that there was a group of figures, some of them women, waiting in the tunnel of the courtyard. Jahan Shah motioned toward them.

"No wonder I stay in town. How they plague me. Always wanting something. They say they come to welcome me. Bah!" The women, two of them, were now standing by the window. "These are the worst," he whispered.

One of the women, in a whining voice that rarely stopped to gulp for air, told a long tale of her husband's blood pressure.

"He will burst," she said.

"You lie," said Jahan Shah. "He eats too much." The woman called on God and the Prophet and struck her breasts. Gruffly, Jahan Shah agreed to take the man back with us to town so that he might see a doctor.

"You will be remembered in our prayers," the woman said.

"If only they would forget me," he mumbled.

The other woman began, her face, runneled as rain-washed earth, raised to the sky, eyes streaming, her hands at her breasts.

"He's gone, gone," she cried, her voice shuddering with grief. "Oh God, he's gone." It was her son, and we thought that he was dead.

"When did you bury him or is it yet to be done?" Jahan Shah hollered out to her.

"Bury him! God forbid. He's not dead. He's gone to the oil fields in the gulf." Would Jahan Shah write him and command him to return. And perhaps a bit of money to help pay for the return. . . .

"We shall see, we shall see," Jahan Shah roared back. "Now go along and leave me in peace."

On they came to the window, Jahan Shah receiving them from the *korsi* like a king in his bedchamber. One old man complained that the local love potions were no longer working for him, and would Jahan Shah bring him something more efficacious from the town. Another wanted a job for his nephew, another a loan. Finally it was over.

"Come," said Jahan Shah. "Let's go and see the animals — a relief from the whining humans." He put the sheepskin coat around my shoulders, and we went out into the muck of the farm courtyard. A little snow now whirled in the wind and we ducked quickly into the stables, dark and warm, smelling of hay — the sheep, at our entrance, thumping their hoofs and bleating. Jahan Shah leaned against a stall while the shepherd moved among the sheep, pulling them around one by one to show the heavy flap of wool and fat that hangs down over the rumps of the local sheep. Sometimes Jahan Shah would lift a flap, as though to gauge its weight. Then he moved over to the sheep that had lambed and, kneeling down, he picked up two of the lambs in his arms and began to rub his cheek against their fleece, whispering to them, tickling them, finally holding them out from himself and laughing at them. He turned to me.

"Did you ever do it to a sheep?" I told him I had not. "I did sometimes as a boy. It wasn't bad. I like the softness." He picked up one of the lambs again, put it between his squatting legs and briefly made the motions of humping, looking back at me and laughing, for he knew I was a little shocked. Then he got up and told the shepherd to drive the sheep out into the farmyard so that he might see them in a better light.

The air now danced with snow, but nonetheless we stood there while Jahan Shah gazed at the sheep and the other animals — some cows and an Arab stallion — brought out for his inspection.

"I should come to the village more often," he said. "I like this," he motioned toward the animals. "I like looking at them." Then he glanced at me and noticed that a light cap of snow had formed on my head. He came over and brushed it off and said, "Come along. We'll have our lunch."

Lunch was a pot of stew, bread and cheese, and greens. When we finished, Jahan Shah lay back and moaned.

"Yes," I said. "It was a good lunch."

"No," he said. "It's not that, it's this." He pulled away the comforter and put his hands between his legs. "Look. It's stiff. I could do with a woman now — " He stopped. "But that's a surprise — for later, a surprise for you."

"What surprise?" I asked.

"For later," he repeated, and then he shifted down sidewise and full length under the comforter, pulling it over his head. "Now we sleep."

We woke to find it almost dark, the courtyard luminous with the snow which had fallen while we slept. Jahan Shah gave an enormous yawn, stretched, and then violently shook his head as if to shake the sleep out of it.

"Do this," he said. "It will freshen you," and he leaned over and scooped up the snow from the doorsill and buried his face in it. Then he threw back the comforter. "Come along. We will go and see my agent at his shop." As I was putting on my coat he took it from me and gave

119

me his sheepskin. "I will wear yours and you mine, for you are not accustomed to this cold and need the heavier coat."

"It's not far," he said, as we came out into the lane, "not worth the jeep." We went along through the swirling snow, coming soon to the street which straggled off, forlorn and dark, into the winter night. Only here and there a lantern in some shop threw onto the snow an oblong of amber light.

It was in one of these patches of light that we noticed a tall, unsteady figure coming in our direction. Suddenly, as if just seeing us, the figure bolted forward, calling out, "Jahan Shah, my king, my king."

"It's Abdola, the minstrel," Jahan Shah said. "He plays at the local weddings and such things." The minstrel was now up to us and had pulled Jahan Shah's hand to his lips. He was a wild-looking old fellow, all bones and eyes, a mane of wavy, grey hair falling to his shoulders. Looking at him, I thought of Akbari the jester.

"You're still bawling your rubbishy ballads, are you, Abdola?" Jahan Shah said, and then he leaned forward and buttoned the top button of the old man's coat. "Take care of yourself or you won't be here, when the time comes, to deafen my wedding guests." The old man stepped back and did a little caper, the head down and to one side, and I saw his profile then, the line as pure as some old drachma's Alexander.

"Let me play for you tonight," he said, coming forward again and taking Jahan Shah's hand. Then he turned to me and bowed, "And for your guest. It's been a cold winter. I'm starving to death."

"Yes," said Jahan Shah, "we can use you tonight, especially tonight. Here," and he gave the old man a bill. "Go buy yourself a drink. You play better drunk than sober."

We went on then to the agent's shop, a narrow, whitewashed slice of a place, simple and uncluttered, the merchandise — soap, sugar, tobacco, tea, and such things — packaged in plain brown paper and stacked in rows in recessed arches. A short counter, opposite the door, had a scale and brass pans of colored candies on it. Behind this, filling the rear end of the place, ran a carpeted, raised platform. At one end stood a little desk on six-inch legs, an elderly man sitting cross-legged in front of it working an abacus. This was the agent. As soon as he saw Jahan Shah, he hopped off the platform and came running to greet us. He was a little, strong-looking old man with beetling white eyebrows and quick and happy eyes. It was obvious at once that Jahan Shah liked him very much, chucking him under the chin and holding his hand as we went up to the platform to sit around the brazier.

We had not been there long — talking of farm matters, drinking tea — when peasants began to enter the shop, big men in black, wide-legged trousers, their brown felt cloaks lightly mantled with snow. Each, approaching the platform, held Jahan Shah's hand for a moment between his own two hands — the greeting of fealty — and I realized then that they were Jahan Shah's peasants and that apparently a meeting of some kind had been arranged.

After inquiries concerning everyone's health plus many expressions of affection and respect, the gathering got down to business, a question concerning the division of certain crops between Jahan Shah and the peasants. I had witnessed these landlord-peasant disputes before, but never had I seen a performance of such virtuosity as that delivered by Jahan Shah. The peasants, who wanted a greater share of the crop than Jahan Shah wanted to give, were subjected to both blandishment and abuse, and in many forms. He embraced them, he kicked them, he held their hands, he snarled, he laughed, he yelled, he scoffed. The crescendo of all these various thrusts was reached when Jahan Shah, head high, thumb and forefinger together and thumping his chest, would bring his face within an inch of the peasant and then bellow like a maddened bull. This would be followed by his turning away, head in his hands, shoulders heaving as if he were about to weep. And then he would mutter in a broken voice such phrases as: ". . . the ingratitude . . . such faithlessness . . . after all that I have done for them . . ."

In such a fashion negotiations broke down often. When this occurred, the agent, and sometimes passers-by drawn in from the street, would mediate — and usually with success, for Iranians are hardly adverse to compromise.

Thus the scene in the shop gradually quieted, and finally Jahan Shah was sitting calmly on the edge of the platform stroking the hand of an old peasant who squatted at his feet and to whom, only moments before, he had been most abusive.

"I am very fond of him," he said to me, giving the old man's hand a tug, "though the poor fellow is a little mad —," he lowered his voice, "— took a sickle once to his brother, lopped the head right off." He paused, gazing out pensively at the snow-flecked night, and then abruptly his mood changed, as if the night reminded him of something, and he moved over next to me, his eyes bright with excitement. His arm around my shoulder, he put his mouth to my ear, biting and licking it a little as he did, and whispering that now he would tell me the surprise. At the house, he said, he had a woman for us for the night.

Jahan Shah would talk no more about the matter until we were back at the house and under the *korsi* having dinner.

"I keep her as a maid servant," he explained, "so that when I come from town — well, so that I may have a woman here." He smiled and scratched himself. "She's no great beauty but I like her, slippery and quick as a little lynx. She —" he stopped, for Abdola the minstrel was tapping at the window.

Jahan Shah got up and brought the old man in. Under his arm he carried a *tar*, the Iranian double-bellied lute. Leading him to the rear of the *korsi* room, Jahan Shah opened a door into another room, hardly larger than a closet, in which there were a pallet and a lighted charcoal brazier.

"Now go in there," Jahan Shah said, pushing the old man toward the door, "and play a bit on and off — and softly mind you — until you see from under the door that I've blown out the lamp. Then get yourself to sleep and we'll see you in the morning." The old man gently struck a chord, a bare ripple of sound.

"Have a pleasant evening, gentlemen," he said, bowing to us, and then he went into the little room and closed the door.

Jahan Shah took down a camel's-hair cloak from a peg on the wall.

"I want to check the lambing," he said, "and then I'll bring her." When he opened the door to go, I could hear the wind booming through the tunnel of the courtyard and for an instant I felt its blast against my cheek. Then the door closed, it was warm again, and I lay back wondering about the girl and listening to Abdola's muffled plucking of the lute.

In a few minutes they were there — Jahan Shah behind her, tall, his hand on her shoulder — the two of them coming through the door in a gust of snow. She wore Jahan Shah's camel's-hair cloak and her head was bound tightly, cloche-like, in a chador, the face exposed. Jahan

Shah was right: she was no beauty — the eyes and nose too big for the narrow, peaked little face, her color poor, almost to yellowness. She stood there, saying nothing, looking at me out of her big, staring eyes with a gaze in which there was a touch of fear but also much of cool inspection.

"This is Fatima Khanom," Jahan Shah said, grave and courtly, and then to her, "Your cloak," and she raised her arms and let it fall into his hands. Beneath she was wearing an old, blue plush jacket, gingham pantaloons, and a gold ankle bracelet. Her shirt, low cut as the shirts of peasant women often are to make nursing easy, left her big and flaccid breasts partly exposed. She crossed her hands against herself and then, laughing, took them away and got into the *korsi* beside me. I saw then that she was tattooed, a blue spot high on either cheek.

Meanwhile Jahan Shah was groping in his valise, coming out at last with a bottle of perfume. He got into the *korsi* beside her and held out the perfume in the palm of his hand. She snatched it from him, wrenched off the top, took big sniffs, and then, putting a little on her finger, rubbed the end of his nose with it.

"You animal," she said, "you need it more than I." He laughed and slapped at her head, and she slapped back at him. Then she turned to me. There was that look, as there had been before, of inspection, though this time the hint of fear was gone and she smiled a little. Again she poured a few drops of the perfume onto her finger, lightly touched my cheek with it, and then touched it to herself at the base of her throat.

We lay, the three of us in a row, the comforter tucked under our chins — like children, somehow, put into one big bed — talking, sometimes stopping to listen to Abdola's lute. Jahan Shah reported to Fatima on his efforts to find her a husband in the town. It was difficult, he said, but he didn't mention why; nor did he need to, for we all knew that any man who would marry a girl who was not a virgin would probably not be of good character himself.

"We shall work it out somehow," Jahan Shah said in a concluding way, as though he wanted to get on to something else. And then I saw from the movement of the comforter that he had begun to tickle her legs with his toes. In a moment — and again like children, roughhousing children — all three of us were tussling, Fatima pinching and jabbing at us, biting when she could. Finally, tired, calling "time" as it were, we all lay back, panting a little and laughing. Then Jahan Shah got up from the *korsi.* "I want to check the lambing one more time," he said, and putting on the camel's-hair cloak, he went out.

The girl then turned to me to say that I was the first foreigner she had ever known. Did I have a sister, she asked. And when I told her yes, she asked a string of questions: was she beautiful; how often did she bathe; could she sew; did she veil herself; and finally, was she married or did she have a fiancé. When I had answered all her questions, she let her head drop onto my shoulder and we lay there, not talking, listening to the wind crooning its accompaniment to Abdola's lute.

Jahan Shah was back in a few minutes, coming through the door in a roar of wind.

"Now," he said, throwing off the cloak, and he was beside us in a leap, on his knees and pulling Fatima's plush jacket off her shoulders. The tussling began again, Fatima quick and fierce, not playing, her knees and elbows jabbing us and hurting. Finally, though she slithered in our grasp like a maddened cat, we had her arms and legs pinned down. "Now, my girl," Jahan Shah said, "now we have you." With a sudden down-thrust of her head, she bit into his wrist. Yelping with the pain, he cursed her, and she laughed. He raised his hand then, about to strike her, when she pointed to the window. We looked and saw that the wind had changed and now the snow was striking the glass, each flake spreading, as it struck, into a ragged star. While we watched, Fatima began to hum quietly to herself and at the same time to gently play with us. I looked down at her. Her eyes were closed, her face quiet, and with that quietness a kind of beauty had come into it.

"Fateh, Fateh," Jahan Shah said, using the diminutive of her name, his voice trembling on the syllables like the plucked strings of the lute. Raising himself a little, he blew out the lamp and the lute stopped; there was only the night, ourselves, and the pelting snow against the glass.

Journal V

Wıтн Mᴀᴍᴅᴀʟɪ off on pilgrimage, Khanom and I have more chance to talk. The other evening I went down the cypress alley to sit at the millstone table and watch the moon come up. After a time, Khanom appeared leading two sheep by long chains. Only the oval of her face and her arm in its bright blue sweater sleeve caught what light was left. It occurred to me that if one saw that face across a room at a party in New York one would think — what a striking woman! We take her too much for granted here.

I asked her to sit down, which she gladly did, for she loves to talk and also is lonesome for Mamdali. It came out that she had sold the sheep. I knew that dealers had been around all day, prodding and poking at the sheep, and there had been much prolonged and scrappy bargaining. Iranian men do not like to bargain with Iranian women; the latter can be very difficult. In any event, she had sold them and at her price, and further she had known she would, for she had dreamt the whole affair the night before. These dreams! Is there an Iranian who doesn't heed them?

Curious to know if her interpretations differed from Mamdali's, I asked her what she considered to be bad dreams, or dreams, at any rate, portending bad fortune. Nothing, she said, could be quite so bad as for the dreamer to put on red clothes, though red shoes were bad as well.

"When I have such dreams," she went on, "I go in the morning to the water spigot in the yard, turn it on, and say, 'O water, carry my bad dream to the top of the black mountain.' " Where, I asked, was the black mountain? She pondered for a moment and then said that she wasn't altogether certain.

We then went on to good dreams. There was nothing better than to see a fish in water, though a wheel turning, on the ground or in the sky, was also an excellent omen. Dancing, too, especially when accompanied by levitation. In fact, shortly before her engagement to Mamdali she had dreamt that she was dancing in the sky.

This dream led to some details of that engagement which I had not heard before. I only knew that, for a boy in his position, Mamdali had paid her a very high *mehriyeh,* the money which the man must pledge before marriage and which goes to the wife in the event of divorce or death.

"I was first loved," she said, "by a boy who worked with my father. His mother sent cloth and candies. I didn't touch the candies; they were eaten by my married sisters."

"Oh?" I said.

"Yes, of course," she said, as though I was a little dense, "so that he would know I didn't want him." She laughed and gave a shake to one of the sheep chains. "He was a noble boy but not pretty, and he wore a fat turban, not becoming to him, being so short. Anyway, I did not want a boy who wore a turban. My dream was a boy who dressed in coat and trousers and used perfume."

"And Mamdali?" I asked.

"O my!" she replied and pulled her chador across her face.

It seemed that Mamdali and some of his friends had spent six months on the roof of her father's house — they were distant relatives — hiding out from the conscription. Everyone in the village knew that he was on the roof, but they could truthfully report they hadn't seen him. So there he roosted for six months with little to do but look down on Khanom and her sisters weaving in the court-yard.

"It was improper," she said, "for there in my own court-yard I didn't wear a chador, of course, and he could see my face. For six months he did nothing but call down poems and sing to me." She folded her hands in her lap. "He was very handsome."

At some point inquiries were made. She had cousins who had been camel drivers with Mamdali and they reported that he was good-tempered.

"So," she said, throwing out her hand, the implication being that a girl could not wish for more than a boy who was not only handsome but good-tempered as well. In time his mother sent candies and cloth. Khanom ate the candies and had the cloth made into a new chador, and the date for the marriage was settled. A few weeks before the marriage, however, she decided that "for fun" she would tell everyone that she did not think she wanted Mamdali after all. When she related this to me, there came into her voice something of the tone I had heard earlier in the day when she bargained with the dealers. "He and his mother threatened to kill themselves," she concluded with satisfaction.

She had one more thing to tell me, an incident which had taken place after her marriage.

"I told Mamdali that I sometimes become angry, and that I cannot become angry with the floors and walls and so would have to become angry with him, and that he must understand this and forgive me." She laughed. "And he does, usually."

By now the moon had risen, turned directly on us like a great floodlight. Khanom gathered her chador around her and took up the chains. We started back. At the door she bade me good night.

"Dream well tonight," she said. "Perhaps you'll see the turning wheel — and I shall see Mamdali."

The mulberry season is on. From the old days when Iran produced much silk the trees are all over the country. Iranians love mulberries. A friend in town tells me, and seriously, that the outpatient departments of hospitals are overflowing throughout the mulberry season with people who have fallen from the trees and suffered some kind of injury.

We have only one mulberry tree, but it is old and large and still bears plentifully. Every morning Khanom goes to the tree and spreads her chador under it. Then the children hit the branches with long poles or Mamdali climbs up into the branches and shakes the berries down. How cool and sweet they are. We shall eat them now every morning for a month.

A few days ago I went over the mountains to Hussain Malek's place. The Arab mare has something wrong with her, and I thought Malek, having lots of horses, might give me some idea of how to treat her.

When I arrived I found that Malek had another guest, a minor khan from somewhere west whose name was Ali Mordad. He was a lump of a man with no teeth, an ugly bulb of a nose, and he dressed in the usual black and white chasuble of his tribe, a dirty silk sash around his waist. I didn't like him much. He went about with a certain irritable self-importance and there was something brute about him which frightened me a little. But my host seemed to take him as a joke, at least in part — the other part, distaste. As the day passed, I learned enough from Malek to understand both his reactions.

Ali Mordad in his youth had been well known in those parts for his vanity and good looks. The vanity had taken one especially preposterous turn. Malek told me that in the old days it was customary for a great khan to keep a white donkey fitted with a special kind of saddlebag. This saddlebag was divided into many little pockets and each contained an article of the khan's more personal effects: his tea and sugar, perfume, looking glass, comb and nail-file, and other such things. Ali Mordad was not a great khan and thus not entitled to the white donkey and saddlebag. His vanity, however, led him to arrange for the next best effect. He had a white vest made with pockets like the saddlebag's and put it on one of his servants. The whole countryside had laughed.

It was things of this sort that made Malek consider him a joke. But there was another side which was not so funny. The man was a killer, and if he had been the old-style American outlaw, he would have had six notches on his gun.

After dinner Malek, Ali Mordad, and I went up on the roof to take our tea and smoke. There the reason for Ali Mordad's visit came out. He had come to buy three mares. This puzzled me, for tribesmen consider it bad form to ride a mare. So I inquired of him why he was buying them. He laughed in his ugly way and then told me the story.

One day, about a year and a half before, he had gone with some of his men, and his wife, to visit his father-in-law's camp. While they were there, some other guests arrived and the father-in-law asked his daughter, Ali Mordad's wife, to serve tea to them. Ali Mordad objected: his wife would serve no other man's guests. The father-in-law insisted: after all, the girl was his daughter. Ali Mordad, in response, threatened to brand the girl if she disobeyed him. Dismissing this as an idle threat, the father-in-law persuaded the girl to serve the guests. When Ali Mordad found out what had happened, he carried out his threat, branding the poor girl in ten places. She then ran off to her father's tent, Ali Mordad following, and in the fracas which followed he shot the father-in-law to death. With the aid of his men he got away and since that time had been living as an outlaw.

But now a reconciliation had been arranged, and part of the terms of the settlement had been three mares — mares since the issue in the quarrel had been a woman. In addition he had been required to give in recompense some land, a girl for marriage from his family, and two donkey-loads of sugar.

I was curious to know how the actual reconciliation would take place. He offered the information casually, as though the ceremony was a usual one for him. He and his men, bringing with them the promised girl, the mares, the two donkey-loads of sugar, would ride to the dead man's camp. As the men approached, the camp minstrels would begin to play mourning music. Arriving at the camp, Ali Mordad — with a scrap of black cloth from his tent around his neck — would join in the mourning keens, keening louder than the rest, and would go among his own men begging for token contributions of money, which would be added to the other indemnities he had brought. He would then present his sword to the dead man's eldest son, and they would exchange the kiss of peace. With that, expiation done, festive music would replace the dirge and the camp would rejoice.

The next morning Ali Mordad, having purchased the mares, was ready to start off for the dead man's camp. He had about ten men with him, the sugar-laden donkeys, and the girl, quite hidden beneath a plum-colored chador, astride a fine black stallion. Just as he was about to leave, one of his men brought him the piece of black tent cloth. He slapped it around his neck. Then they all rode off into the mountains.

The Pilgrimage

NOT FAR from our village mosque stood a little shrine called Baba Abbas. Baba Abbas was a fourteenth-century theologian whose tomb was used in the past — perhaps is sometimes today — to test the veracity of witnesses. According to Mamdali, if the witnesses lied, "they suddenly burst and their bowels gushed out." The shrine itself had a dome like a high, white, conical hat, and its portal was a cove of old blue tile set into a rectangle of buff brick. Inside stood the tomb, surrounded by a wooden railing. Lamps, which gave the only light, burned on it, and tied to the railings were bits of votive cloth. The walls were sooted black from the smoking lamps, and there was in the air of the place a whiff of tallow and frankincense. Outside in the sleepy little square there was often a nut seller, his big brass pans along one wall, and perhaps a woman drawing water from the public pump. Now and then, like walk-ons in a play, people would pass across the square on their way somewhere.

It was here one afternoon, while trying to make a sketch of the portal, that I ran into Mamdali's cousin, Masht Hassan, the shoemaker. Looking up from my sketch, I saw him standing in the gloom of the shrine doorway. He was a tall, emaciated man with sharp shoulder blades poking up through his old coat. The face too was lean, haggard, but the eyes were big and soft. He looked like a gentle Cassius.

Masht Hassan blinked in the brightness of the sun and then, focusing, he recognized me. His hand across his heart in greeting, he came and squatted by my side, looking at the sketch, tilting his head this way and that. I had, he said, the hand of a master — there was no doubt of that. By now, having lived some years in Iran, I was used to such compliments. They bore little relation to the truth, yet in their wish to please they were entirely sincere, and I had grown, the truth being so often what it is, to like these generous, well-turned lies.

For a time we talked of this and that: Mamdali, the weather, the shrine itself. Then Masht Hassan, touching my knee, asked if I had visited any of the great shrines of the country. When I replied that I had not, he began to tell me something of his own experiences as a pilgrim.

His shop, he said, and as I well knew, was more often closed than not since he enjoyed going off on pilgrimage so much. He had traveled to all the great shrines of Iran and Iraq, some several times over. His first pilgrimage had been made at the age of fourteen to the Shrine of Imam Reza at Meshed in northeastern Iran. Imam Reza, one of the early leaders of Shiah Islam, is especially beloved by Iranians, and his shrine is said to be among the most dazzling buildings in the East. The pilgrimage was made with a group of cousins and friends biking, and it had taken them two weeks. One evening, en route, they stopped to camp by a pool in the mountains. After they had settled themselves in, one of Masht Hassan's cousins sneaked a bottle of wine out of his kit. Wine, as well as other alcohol, is forbidden by religious law, but nonetheless they drank it because, Masht Hassan said, the place was so poetic. The wine, however, led to other things, for they all got a little drunk, stripped to their skins, and swam in the pool. Nudity, too, is strictly forbidden by religious law.

To me these transgressions seemed, at least in some degree, to debase the pilgrimage. From what I knew of pilgrims, in Ireland and Mexico, they were people who climbed on their knees up rocky mountains. There was neither wine on the way nor horseplay in a pool. "So be it," said Masht Hassan when I asked him, and the implication was that human nature being what it is, transgressions are now and then inevitable, and not only inevitable but a desirable spice. I was to find out what he meant when, the next week, he and I went off on pilgrimage together.

Since I didn't have the time to go as far away as Meshed, the shrine that Masht Hassan chose for our pilgrimage was the major shrine of our area. We met that morning at a teahouse in the town which served as the station for the shrine bus. I was first introduced to the driver. He was sitting on a stool near the bus, sucking up a glass of tea, a pockmarked little fellow with a gold tooth and a black beret pulled down over his eyes. "You honor us," he said to me, throwing his arm out toward the bus as though it were the state carriage. "Please ascend."

The bus, though old and small, was painted up very smartly in red, green, and white. Inside there were artificial flowers in holders at either side of the windshield, an oleograph of the Prophet above, charms strung on a cord, and, along the dashboard, decals of naked big-rumped ladies.

We sat down in our seats to wait until a few more passengers came along, enough at least to cover the gas for the trip, for this, rather than a schedule, determined the time of departure. At last, with ten or twelve aboard, we started out. There were some women with sick infants, going to the shrine to ask for their cure; several groups of people who, from their holiday mood and all the pots and lunch canisters, appeared to be off to the shrine for a picnic; and finally, sitting in the back of the bus, two young toughs, bawling their eyes out.

"What's wrong?" I whispered to Masht Hassan.

"Perhaps someone in their family is sick; perhaps in sorrow for their sins they are going to the shrine to repent; perhaps disappointment in love. It is hard to say — God knows. We cry often and easily and for many reasons."

Masht Hassan brought out a little muslin bag with drawstrings and poured into my hand a pile of roasted wheat and melon seeds, a staple on any Iranian journey. By now some of the picnickers had moved back to comfort the bawling toughs. The driver talked to a friend who had come along for the ride. A woman nursed her child. Masht Hassan told me to look out the window; it was spring, and on the branches of the fruit trees, beyond the high clay walls, there was a faint blur of green.

As we went along, I heard from Masht Hassan something of the curious history of the shrine. It seemed that, some years before, a chest containing certain documents had been found in an exhumed grave. The documents purported to give the location of the burial places of several holy women, among them a member of the Prophet's family. The document stated that this woman's remains would be found in the middle of a sheepfold near a certain village outside the town. Investigation was made, and a grave, it is said, was found. Not long after, the shrine was built at the place.

Masht Hassan went on, however, to say that the land surrounding the shrine belonged, and had belonged before the grave was discovered, to a certain family. The teahouses, fruit stall, and other shops adjacent to the shrine were now under their control, as, for that matter, was the bus on which we were traveling. Masht Hassan left it at that. The implication that perhaps this family had planted the documents was not made, though nonetheless it was somehow there. But I knew that it made

little difference because I knew as well that for Masht
Hassan, as for most Iranians, truth was a matter of mood
and wish and dream, not a matter of objective fact. For
the pilgrims, the bones of this holy woman lay in the
sheepfold if it pleased and comforted them to think so;
and, as I was to learn, it did.

Soon after Masht Hassan finished his story, we came
into view of the shrine itself. It lay in rather open country, a squarish enclosure of clay walls with the dome at
one end — a great bulb of turquoise tile with yellow arabesques floating around it and, at the top, a gold finial
flashing the sun. Inside the enclosure we found a courtyard with trees and, down the center, a stone water channel. Around the perimeter there were little verandaed
rooms where pilgrims from distant places might stay the
night. Since it was a weekday and a morning, the courtyard was not crowded. This disappointed Masht Hassan.
It was, he said, a better "show" when there were more
people.

But it seemed to me that there was show enough. The
picnickers from the bus had gone to join other picnickers
under the trees. Blankets were spread, the samovars set
up; people were talking, playing with their children, or
stretched out asleep. Some sideburned boys in fashion-
able suits, cigarettes hanging from their lips, walked
around the courtyard taking photographs. In one of the
little verandaed rooms there was a group of elderly clerics
with goat beards and tightly knotted turbans, smoking
their water pipes and looking like wizened, embittered old
pirates.

We walked down to the end of the courtyard and
through the arch that led to the tomb. It lay, a long,
inscribed slab, in a grill beneath the dome. Sprawled at
its base were the toughs from the bus, their heads against

the grill, sobbing without restraint. When we came near, one of them rubbed the tears from his eyes to see who was there, and then went back to his grief. On the other side of the tomb, several women sat on the ground in the folds of their chadors, holding out to the tomb their swathed infants. In one corner an old woman rested back on her knees, her hands palm downwards on her thighs, her face, a crackled parchment, raised and still, the eyes half-closed in trance. While we stood there, there began from the women and the toughs what sounded like a litany, a kind of choric plea. It rose like a wave into anguish, then fell again to low, disjointed sobs. To comfort them, Masht Hassan took from his pocket a bottle of rosewater and, pouring some of it onto his hands, he went and patted the faces of the toughs, and then went to the women, who cupped their hands to receive it. Shadows moved in across the floor. It was the fashionably suited boys. They stood by the tomb, heads down, their hands pressed hard against their eyes.

Outside again, in the sun of the courtyard, Masht Hassan suggested that we visit the mill that stood near the shrine. It had, he said, a tower from which we might look down into an early-blooming orchard. Also, he thought that there might be something else there I would enjoy.

The mill was a huddle of dark, cavelike little rooms, the corners drifted with flour, the whole place trembling in the rumble of the mill wheel, which turned somewhere deep below it. A spiral staircase in a corner of one room brought us out onto the roof of the tower. Below lay the walled orchard of almond bloom, drifting in the wind, throwing its fragrance up to us. Far beyond stood the town, its domes half-hidden in the greenery like robins' eggs. The mountains ended the view in big blue scoops against the sky.

Masht Hassan was very proud of this view. "God indeed is great," he soberly said. And for a few moments we looked out at it all. Then he winked and took my hand. "Come along; there is another pleasure too."

I had noticed when we entered the mill a smell like burning rubber but sweet, an unpleasant smell, yet with something good in it. As we passed from one room to another the smell grew stronger. Finally, we reached what was hardly more than a cell except for a small, arched, paneless window which opened right out onto the almond boughs. Here two old men sat on a scrap of carpet by the window, a brazier between them, one of them holding to his lips a long pipe with a china ball at the end. As I had thought, it was opium I smelled.

The old men got up, greeted us, and gestured toward the carpet for us to join them. It turned out that they were acquaintances of Masht Hassan, merchants from the bazaar who had decided to take the day off to visit the shrine and to see the almond blossoms. They had come at dawn with a pot of sheep's head, which, having prayed at the tomb, they ate for breakfast under the trees in the court. They were quick, clean, birdy old men, the white hair on their hard brown skulls clipped short, and there was something in their way with each other that made them seem like brothers or like two men who had known and liked each other all their lives.

We sat chatting with them for a little while, and then one of the old men, nodding at me, confirming in fact what I secretly wished, began to prepare the pipe for me. First he put the china ball at its end among the ashes to warm it; then from a nickel case he took a stick of opium and cut off a piece about the size of a pea. Next, taking the pipe from the ashes and feeling the ball to see if it was warm enough, he began to plunge out the little hole in its top with a pearl stickpin which hung on a chain from the pipe. It was ready now for the opium, which he pasted down over the hole. There, in contact with the warmth, the opium softened a little like wax. I took the pipe, and at the same time the old man fished with the steel tongs among the coals for a suitable chunk. Finding one, he held it barely above the opium while I blew hard into the pipe. The stream of air, passing up through the hole and the opium, turned the coal red, and in its heat the opium began to blob and sizzle. It was the sign to inhale, and I took in the smoke as deeply as my lungs could pull it. When I had finished, the old man poured me a little glass of scalding tea. Leaning back and drinking it, I looked out into the almond branches. They told me that I would be at peace all day, remember the almond branches, and sleep well that night.

The old men and Masht Hassan talked on, gossiping and telling stories, occasionally asking if I was comfortable, offering more tea and opium. I was content. Nothing could have been more pleasant than the little domed room with its feeling of being a secret chamber, the one arched window opening on the almond branches, the lulling rumble of the mill, the opium beginning to work its peace. At one point, Masht Hassan broke off a sprig of almond blossom and gave it to me, a memento of my day at the shrine, he said.

And what did I think of the shrine, one of the old men asked, and did we have such places in America? I told him that by and large we did not.

"No doubt you have your own ways of worship," he replied. "The different races and classes of men have their different ways, some outlandish, I'm sure, but all, if well intended, acceptable to God." And then he told us the story of Moses and the shepherd:

One day Moses, walking in the fields, came upon a
shepherd. The shepherd was praying to God as if God
were another shepherd: "O God! When at night you are
weary, I shall rub your feet and I shall bring you fresh
cold water and I shall pick the burrs from your beard and
hair."

"Clod of a shepherd," said Moses. "Don't you know
that God is all-powerful, that he does not know weariness
or thirst, and that in his kingdom there are no burrs?"

Then God appeared to Moses and chastised him, saying: "Moses, it is your mission to bring my creatures closer
to me, not to drive them away, beyond their understanding, as you have done with this poor shepherd."
And Moses repented, and the shepherd was consoled.

"So we worship in our own ways, and isn't it right?" the
old man ended, cocking his eyebrows. "Here in this
place, for example, it's a woman we honor. Does that
strike you as strange?" I told him it did not. "No, I suppose not. After all you have the noble lady, Mariam —
'Mary' you call her? — the mother of your great Prophet.
Anyway, what is more natural than that we, at any rate,
should have many women among our saints, for what really is more precious in this world than a woman?" He
slapped his thigh. "My God, as saints or plain women,
how we love them — and to the end. Look at this old
grandfather." He nodded toward his friend. "You know
that he took himself a third wife last year, a fine fat girl of
seventeen!" And laughing, he leaned over and patted the
other old fellow's crotch. "Yes, to the end. And do you
know —" he stopped and looked at us. "If I have your
permission; it is an indelicacy — but anyway, they say that
on his wedding night he became so excited that he bit the
poor girl, there, in her place." The friend protested, flat-

tered. Masht Hassan clucked his tongue, shocked and
delighted. All three of them started off on a round of
stories.

By now it was almost noon, and Masht Hassan invited
the old gentlemen to lunch with us in the shrine court.
We walked back through the dark little rooms, out into
the sunlight. A voice from somewhere in the shrine sang
out the midday call to prayer.

At the water channel in the court, Masht Hassan and
the old men took off their shoes and rolled up their
sleeves in order to perform the ablutions required before
prayer. These completed, they stood, facing Mecca, and
began the bowings that accompany prayer — bowing first
from the waist, then kneeling and touching the forehead
to a prayer stone on the ground, sitting back on the heels,
and bowing again to the ground. "Besmellah, Arrahman,
Arrahim" ("O God, the most merciful and compassionate"), they intoned.

We took our lunch on the scrap of carpet under the
trees. There was yogurt, rice, spinach cakes, bread and
cheese, and radishes, and, for dessert, some dates. We
ate it all with our hands from a common tray and drank
commonly from a big blue bowl of water.

Before beginning lunch we had asked the two toughs
from the bus, who were sitting nearby, to join us, but out
of manners they had refused. When it came time for tea
we asked them again, and this time they accepted. We
learned that they were brothers and had been in some
kind of family fight, and in the fracas had injured their
father so badly that he had to be taken to a hospital. As a
penance, and in their remorse, they had come to the
shrine to gain forgiveness. There was no sign now of
their tears. They had emptied themselves, and they
talked to us like men who are very tired but at rest. The

old men gave them a brief and gentle lecture. Had they done *ashti*, the ritual of reconciliation? Yes, they had gone to the hospital and kissed their father's feet, and he had kissed them on both cheeks. They had promised him, as a kind of penance, a visit to the shrine and a sheep to be killed and given to the poor. Both parts of the penance had now been carried out. "So," said Masht Hassan, patting their knees, "the whole thing is in the past, forgiven and forgotten." They thanked him.

After lunch we went back to the mill to sleep. The old men led us to a narrow bank between the millstream and the mill. It had a good covering of turf, and some willows laced the place with shade. In the sound of the flowing water, the willows streaming in the breeze, we soon went off to sleep.

When I woke up, Masht Hassan was filling the kettle to make tea. Waiting for it to boil, we stripped to our shorts and took a dip in the millstream. Then we came out and drank the tea, sitting on the edge of the bank, beyond the shade, so that the sun might dry us.

The old men and Masht Hassan wanted to make a last visit to the tomb before we returned to the city. I waited for them in the shrine court. The sun by now had passed to the far side of the dome, and so the chamber beneath it was in darkness except for the lamps that burned above the tomb. Masht Hassan and the old men were lost somewhere in the gloom of the place. I waited. And then I saw them, one by one, move into the tomb's faint light and kneel to kiss the grill. They came out then, together, smiling. The pilgrimage was over. It had been, it seemed to me, a most refreshing day, both God and man remembered.

Journal VI

Yesterday the mad man, a blind boy with him, came to the back gate to beg. I told Khanom to bring them in and feed them well, and I gave her money to give them, too. I suppose I thought that by doing this I might make up in part for what happened last week.

I was coming in the gate when a shepherd boy came up to me to beg. He was a terrible sight, his eyes filled with mucus, flies clotted there and at his nostrils. Head down, half crying, half moaning, he put his hand out. I gave him a bit of change and then hurried to unlock the gate. But he pulled at my coat, wanting more, his head still down, accepting the flies. I had not given him much, but the only other thing I had was a bill, which seemed too much to give a beggar. I told him to go away. He stumbled a little. I fled through the gate.

All week I have been haunted by the look of him and by what I didn't do — not giving him the bill, not bringing him in to have Khanom bathe his eyes. So I was glad when the mad man came with this blind boy so that I might feed them and give them money.

The mad man went off after his dinner, but the boy stayed, saying he wanted to thank Khanom by singing for her. I went out to talk with him. He was in his middle teens, tall, lanky, and very dark, his eyes white, like blobs of phlegm. He kept his head raised high as if some light came through from the sky, and when I asked him if this was so he said it was.

He told us a little about himself, that he was from the town and that he had "a thousand fathers," meaning that his mother was a whore. He said too, though as if teasing us, that before going blind he had been a parachutist, a race-car driver, and a cowboy, and privately, behind his hand, he whispered to me that he was a great favorite of a rich and beautiful woman in the town because what he had was "as big as an eggplant." He seemed so gay, telling us his dreams. It was as though, free from the sight of the world, he had in a way a greater freedom, that he roamed where he wanted in his darkness.

The talk went on so late that I decided he should stay the night, and so I told Khanom to put some comforters out for him on the *mahtabi*. He thanked us and then turned away and began to cry.

He was off this morning while I slept, but Khanom said that before he left he sang to her again.

The other afternoon, while out for a ride, I came on a dervish sitting in a tree. This was a coincidence of sorts, for the night before, while reading the journals of Dr. Fryer, a sixteenth-century traveler in Iran, I happened on this passage: "Most of them [dervishes] are vagabonds and the pest of the nations they live in. All the heat of the day they idle it under some shady tree." And here, four centuries later, was a dervish doing precisely that.

Mamdali shares Dr. Fryer's prejudices concerning dervishes. "They are insidious libertines," he once pronounced. On another occasion he expressed himself more concretely: "If you've an itch at your asshole and you start to give it a scratch, the dervish will think you're going to put your hand in your pocket and give him money."

Yet I have not found them so bad. They come knocking at the gate sometimes, begging — granted — but to give the devils their due, they have on occasion sung for their supper. One once did conjuring tricks, producing baby chicks out of his mouth, and another time an old man recited a long heroic poem for us, illustrating it with a book he had of rough colored cartoons, holding the book up for us to see and turning the pages as he went along.

In any event, I found the dervish in the tree a most agreeable old gentleman and perhaps, too, he may have been what dervishes claim to be, a friend of God.

The tree I found the dervish in is our local holy tree. The trunk, a grey hulk with the girth of a millstone, divides a little way up into three subsidiary trunks, which rise from the main trunk some sixty feet. The branches are a natural aviary, always filled with birds, and deep in the crevices of the trunk there are bees. Women are often there cooking lentil soup, which they offer to anyone who passes by. They do this as a *nazr,* that is, in gratitude for some favor for which they have prayed at the tree and which has been granted.

The dervish, in a red conical hat and with a broad fan of white beard, was sitting cross-legged on a platform that someone had once fitted into the cup formed by the three diverging trunks. He was like a kind of figurehead, sitting there at the heart of the tree, breasting the desert.

"Yah Ali," ("praise Ali") he called out to me as I rode by.

"Yah Ali," I called back.

"Come and take some of this delicious soup, which these good women, remembering God, have made to feed the hungry."

I rode over and said good day to the women. There were half a dozen of them squatting on their haunches by the spring, some of them tending the fire under the pot of soup, the others washing clothes in the pool fed by the spring. The chadors they wore looked as if they had been dyed in blue ink, and as I came near they pulled them over their heads so that they fell like cowls around their faces. Giggling, they jerked their heads in the direction of the old man in the tree, as if to tell me that he was mad, preposterous.

"Come, my son," he called out to me, and he took from a sack by his side a small square of carpet and let it fall to the ground. I went over and sat down, and the women brought me some soup.

The dervish, to my surprise, had all the traditional accouterments of his order; one seldom sees them anymore. Hanging from his girdle on brass chains was a calabash, a kidney-shaped receptacle made from a large hollowed-out gourd, which, all in one, serves as a purse, drinking vessel, and alms box. He had, too, a double-bladed ax damascened in brass and a mace of steel with a stylized horned bull's head at the top. Unlike so many dervishes, he was neatly and cleanly dressed, wearing a green soutane and a camel's-hair cloak. Sitting there on his perch as though levitated, with the conical hat, the grand fan of white beard, the red cheeks, the benign and smiling eyes, he looked half wizard, half Father Christmas.

"Frivolity, frivolity," he said, aiming his mace at the laughing women, one end of it to his eyes, as though sighting through a telescope. "Even here at these holy trees I cannot escape the world's frivolity." He laughed. The women cackled back, swaying in their veils, and he shook his mace at them.

When I asked him where he had come from and where he was going, he answered, "I am in the hands of God as the corpse is in the hands of the washer of the dead: he does with me as he wishes." But then he went on to say that he was on pilgrimage to all the holy trees of Iran. "I lived for some time in a monastery, but — frivolity, frivolity — ," and raising his head he moaned some prayers. Then he took a handful of colored candies out of his calabash, threw a few down to me, and began to pop the rest one by one into his mouth. "Yes, frivolity, and worse," he said. "How the brothers misused the aids! The music, even. Its rhythms should help to move us toward that state where we may see the face of God, but for the brothers it led more often than not to licentious gamboling." He peered down sternly at me from his perch. "And the *dugh-e-hashish* [a drink made of hashish and yogurt water], did it engender a vision of the divine or a vision of the flesh?" He put his hand in the calabash for more of the candies. "There was not even dignity there, the brothers carrying on, throwing melon rinds at one another, playing tricks. And to think they wear the livery of His friends!"

One of the women by the spring stood up, a big figure, her arms, under her chador, folded on her breasts.

"Eh, father?" she called out. "Now don't deceive us. Is it of God you think when you see a girl with a good rump and a waddle, or do you instead shake like the willow with wanting her?" The other women swayed again against each other, laughing.

The old man wagged his mace at them.

"Poor creatures," he said to me. "They can think only of this world." Then he put down his mace and raised his arms into the leaves that hung above him and began to quote from Rumi, the mystic poet:

> "Oh, in the waters of Thy love, O Lord,
> My soul is swimming,
> And ruined all this body's house of clay."

For a moment he was silent, his hands still raised into the leaves. The big woman who had taunted him came over with a bowl of soup and held it up to his perch.

"The body may be made of clay and perhaps ruined a bit, but the belly is still there and yours is big." The old man reached down for the bowl and at the same time put some of the candies into her hand, smiling at her.

Thanking the women for the soup, and getting back on the mare, I wished the dervish a good pilgrimage and good fortune in every way.

"And how could it be otherwise," he crowed back at me, his beard spreading a little with his smile, "for after all, is not my heart the house of God?" And then he went back to his soup.

The Prince

ONE AFTERNOON I went to the airport of the town to meet a friend who was coming from Tehran. During the wait I ran into Madame Pagent, a French woman who had lived in Iran for many years and who was then staying in the town with friends. We sat down to take coffee together and chat about Tehran and the people we knew there.

While we were talking, a man came to our table and greeted Madame Pagent in French. This, together with his tailoring and something boulevardier about him, made me think that he, too, was French. Then we were introduced. He was an Iranian and his name was Shazdeh Ali.

Shazdeh means "prince." Iran is full of princes. The Qajars, who ruled Iran in the nineteenth century, were a most prolific house. Fath'Ali Shah alone had seventy sons, each a prince, and all the male descendants of these sons were princes in turn. Hence the old saying that everywhere in Iran there are camels, lice, and princes. All titles from the Qajar period were outlawed by the succeeding dynasty, and yet here and there, especially in the provinces, the address is sometimes still used. This apparently was the case with Madame Pagent's friend.

We asked the Prince to join us and he did so, the conversation returning to Tehran. He was full of gossip, for he had nine half-brothers there and was well informed indeed. It was a very Iranian conversation, full of jokes and digs and subtle allusions, and yet, despite this, the Prince seemed to me the most un-Iranian Iranian I had ever

met. It was not so much the superficial things — the
Sulka shirt, the Italian gloves, and the old fur-collared
Brooks Brothers tweed coat — as it was his language and
his manner. His English was more than fluent, precise
yet rich, and with a perfect mastery of idiom. As for his
manner, there was a swiftness and ease, an aristocratic ur-
banity and casualness that made me think of him again as
a Frenchman, the kind who works at the Quai d'Orsay
and has a house on the Ile de la Cité.

The Prince invited Madame Pagent and me for tea that
afternoon. She was engaged; I accepted. Then he left
us, slapping his gloves at the palm of his hand and bowing
a little.

In the time left before the plane arrived, Madame
Pagent told me something of the Prince's background.
His father had been Prince-Governor of the province
many years before. The Prince himself had been privately educated until the age of fourteen, when he was
sent to an English public school and from there to Oxford. During the Prince's second year at Oxford, the war
broke out and he was obliged to return to Iran, where, except for brief trips to Europe, he had lived ever since. He
owned a village and country house in the Samonzar Valley, about forty miles east of the farm, and also a house in
town, dividing his time between the two. "He is rather
different from other people," Madame Pagent said. I
later learned that she was right.

The Prince's town house was a large, plain building on
one of the main squares of the town, a second-story
wrought-iron balcony being the only thing to mark its
blank facade. A barefoot country servant let me in and
ushered me up a stairway and along a hall to an open
door. For a moment I thought that by some mistake I
had come to the wrong house. A group of men were sit-

ting cross-legged on the floor of a long room at the end of which, and a little above them, sat the Prince, cross-legged too, on an oval hassock. There was a brazier in front of him, and to his right an elderly woman servant was turning an opium pipe above the coals of the brazier. When he saw me at the door, he got up and, stepping between the sitting men, came toward me. He was wearing wide-legged black trousers — peasant trousers, except that his were made of silk — and a white shirt with a Chinese collar and buttons down the left shoulder. This was the Prince, but not the one I had met at the airport. These were hardly the clothes of a Parisian boulevardier, and his manner as he greeted me and led me to a place near his hassock was in another mode altogether from the flip airport casualness. Now, though cordial, he was subdued and ceremonious.

While I stood, he announced my name to the others and asked if I would be more comfortable in an adjoining room where there were chairs. I told him that I was quite accustomed to the floor and sat down cross-legged on the carpet like the rest. He ordered tea for me and then returned to his conversation with the others, who, I realized now, were his peasants, for the talk was of crops and water.

For the first time I had the chance to look at him carefully. He was in middle age, of average size, broad shouldered but a little sunken in his posture. There were the famous Qajar eyes — as common in this family as the nose among the Hohenzollern — slightly bulging, gleaming eyes with much reverie and languor in them. The cheekbones were high, the lips as set and defined as the lips of a bust. But it was his head, the shape and set of it, that gave him his special style: it was small, compact, and strong, like the head of a bird or reptile. One caught his mood from its movement, and it was often raised and a little thrusting in a kind of happy eagerness.

The conversation went on for a time, and then the Prince turned back to me. He asked questions about the farm and whether there was anything in a general way which he might do for me. After all, I was a foreigner — there might be certain difficulties. In the middle of this he was taken by a fit of coughing. The old woman gave him some tea. When it had quieted him, he spread his hand against his chest and said, "I was shot, you know, several years ago. The bullet is still in my lungs."

It was an explanation of the coughing fit, and yet I felt that in part it had been said for effect. Some people drop names, others drop experiences. He knew very well, I think, the added interest I would take in him because of the remark, and in fact I later inquired about the shooting from some people in the town. It seemed that one day a groom of his had come in from the village and had shot him as he walked across the square outside his house. No one seemed very sure of the reason — some landlord-peasant falling out. In any event, a reconciliation was finally brought about, and by the time I knew the Prince, he had made his assailant the bailiff of his village.

Now and then new visitors were shown into the room. Each was greeted, talked to for a time, and then left on his own with the other guests. Most of the visitors were villagers. One man brought a gunny sack of nuts; another, a brace of ducks. The Prince cracked the nuts and passed them around to us. The ducks he poked and then gave to his cook. One of the visitors was an old man with his grandson, the child receiving more attention from the Prince than all the rest of us put together. He greeted the child as a priest might give a blessing, raising his hands and then bowing to kiss the child's head. Again and again he would turn away from the others to whisper endearments to the child, though always with gravity and gentleness. I was to see it often later, this love of his for children.

Finally it was time for me to go. The Prince, in the meantime, had gone out on the balcony to bargain with a melon seller below on the street, and I went to him there. He was leaning over the railing, joking and haggling with the vendor like a fishwife. Dropping a basket on a rope, he hauled up a melon and gave it to me.

"You must come again," he said, giving my hand a tug as Iranians sometimes do to show their liking of you. I thanked him and told him that I would.

My meeting with the Prince occurred during my first year at the Garden. I was to know him the remainder — almost — of my time in Iran. He was one of the most kindly and engaging men I have ever met. Those were not his only qualities, of course, there was temper and vanity in him, and, as he himself admitted, envy — an envy that sometimes led to malice. But he fought this, literally praying to Hezrat-e-Ali to help him overcome his defect. As for the temper and the vanity, I am sure he thought of these as natural, harmless traits, or it may even be that he considered them virtues integral to a man. Anyway, I would not have had him without the temper and the pride.

During the first years of my friendship with the Prince, I saw him more often at his house in town. His establishment consisted of several sitting rooms, no bedroom — bedrolls anywhere and everywhere taking their place — a courtyard, and large kitchens. The place was run by a good-sized, often changing, very ragtaggle staff. Among those who frequently left, fired or fleeing, but who always came back, there were the following. Jamshid was the Prince's valet, sometimes called the gentleman's gentleman, more often called the Monster. He was a big lout of a boy with happy unfocused eyes, a great head, and a voice of volcanic volume. Jamshid was in "livery." From what Iranian old clothes shop this outfit was acquired, I cannot imagine: it was an American fireman's uniform, though without the hat.

Next there was the Mouse — indeed a mouselike little man with a few pale spikes of moustache and red, wistful eyes. The Mouse cooked, on and off, but his real job was to act as the Prince's procurer. He was an incorrigible thief and was once caught leaving the house in four pairs of the Prince's Sulka underpants. Javad and Ebrahim were general factotums. Javad, a small, tough dandy, acted on occasion as chauffeur; Ebrahim ran messages. This completed what I suppose might be called the lower staff, except for one old man named Abbas who was stone deaf and did nothing.

The upper staff numbered three. The first was that figure found in many old Iranian households — part secretary, part friend, and above all, trouble-shooter. This person in the Prince's household was Aqa Ahmad, a gentle, calm man, a few years younger than the Prince and possibly a relation on the distaff side. Attired in his good English tweeds, an attaché case on his knees, he was forever occupied in trying to solve the financial problems occasioned by the Prince's hopeless extravagance.

Next came Hassan, the Prince's clown. A haggard scarecrow of a man, he was usually drugged to near insensibility by hashish, which he drank in yogurt water. His function, when conscious, was to interpret the Prince's

dreams, to tell him bedtime stories, and on occasion to
leap about — like Akbari, my jester friend — in the performance of salacious pantomimes. Though he appeared
a wild, debauched old fellow, he had in fact much good
sense and kindness.

Then there was Sultaneh, who had been the Prince's
nurse. A well set up old lady, she wore, in the old manner, a white wimple beneath her veil, fastened at the
throat by a gold and turquoise pin which also served as a
charm to keep off the evil eye. She cooked and sewed,
but her special province was the making of excellent preserves. Like Aqa Ahmad, she was a calm presence in the
tempest of that household.

As I have said, these servants, particularly the lower
staff, were constantly coming or going — their places,
when absent, taken by others from the Prince's village or
simply by people picked up from the streets. There were
various reasons for this. For one thing, the servants were
always being either pampered or beaten. They left because of the beatings, came back for the pampering.
There was often good reason for the beatings. The lower
staff were all thieves, constantly borrowing money from
the Prince, or stealing it or anything else which they
thought would not be missed. Another reason, however,
for the frequent changes was that the Prince liked variety.
In the end, however, no servant was ever permanently dismissed, though some of them deserved to be permanently jailed.

There was one other class of persons often in that
household about whom something should be said. The
Prince on the whole, I believe, preferred to take boys and
men to his bed rather than women. Not that he was indifferent to the latter. It was known by everyone that he
had at times kept a mistress, and once someone came

across the Prince on Capri living with a Roman whore. Nonetheless, his usual preference was for males. Some of these were one-night stands procured by the Mouse. But there was also a "steady," a middle-aged greengrocer called the Arab who had a wife and eight children.

Such then was the Prince's household, his court. He could have ruled elsewhere, a man of affairs in some august capacity, for he had excellent connections in the government and at the royal court, but he seemed to prefer the Mouse, the Monster, the clown, old deaf Abbas, and the others — "my dear reprobates," he used to call them.

The Prince's house with its several sitting rooms — five in all, I believe — reflected in part the Prince's liking for variety, but there was another reason, too. The Prince believed in mixing people only when it worked and, as he knew, it frequently did not. A most hospitable man, he often had many guests at his house — and of many different kinds. So there would often be three or four parties going on at once: visitors from his village in one sitting room, kinsmen in another, town riffraff — among whom he had many friends — in still another. Frequently, too, there would be a sitting room of foreigners who, through word of mouth or letters of introduction, would come to visit him.

When one of these four- or five-ring entertainments was going on, it was the practice of the Prince to visit each, checking to see that food and refreshments, and sometimes opium, had been provided, chatting for a little, and then going on to another group. In each sitting room he acted a different role: the suave cosmopolitan among the foreigners, the kinsman among the kinsmen, landlord with the peasants, buddy with the riffraff.

As I remarked before, the Prince was the most

thoroughly Westernized Iranian I have ever known, yet at the same time he was thoroughly Iranian. The secret of this, as I grew to understand, was that as he rarely mixed his guests, so he rarely mixed his different personalities. It is a stock saying among foreigners in Iran that the westernized Iranian is a grotesque, neither this nor that, an exceptionally tricky man to deal with, for one never knows on which level he will respond — the Iranian, the Western, or some mad combination of the two. The Prince, however, had not let this happen. He had apparently decided that it was unwise to confuse things, that a good blend, in view of the clashing ingredients, was in most cases impossible; hence his practice of usually separating his different roles. It was a part of his attraction. He was not a muddle: he was two men, sometimes more, and each of these men was distinct, integral, and interesting.

As time passed I learned to some extent the Prince's lesson for myself — learned to adjust, as did he, to the different norms of the different groups — and thus it was that I was allowed to circulate. After all, another reason for his separation of the groups was that, as a good host, he wanted each group to be comfortable with itself and not to be made self-conscious by the intrusion of an alien presence. When he saw that I was ready to sit on the floor with the peasants, sprawl with the riffraff, and accord the kinsmen the deference they expected, I was free to go to any sitting room I liked, and I did.

My favorite groups were the kinsmen, the riffraff, and sometimes the foreigners. The kinsmen were numerous and varied. There was the cousin who had been the Prince's companion at school in England, an enormously grand man with the manners of a mandarin, but who nonetheless was always tripping both literally and figuratively, his stately progress encountering banana peels all along the way. He had, for example, trouble with his English of a most peculiar kind. For the word he wanted, he would often inadvertently substitute another word, of altogether different meaning, that rhymed with the wanted one. He told me that most Iranians still travel by monkey, meaning donkey, that his wife was sometimes a whore, meaning bore, that he was very fond of virgins, meaning sturgeon.

Another frequent guest was a half-brother whom the Prince referred to as "the fat thing." This half-brother had, for no particular reason, taken to his bed at an early age and was indeed enormous. When he called, he was escorted by three servants, two holding him up on either side, the third carrying his French movie magazines and a box of sweets. They would prop him in a corner full of bolsters and pillows where he would sag like a great sack. He had a whispery kind of voice and spoke English with such an exaggerated upper-class British accent that it was almost impossible to understand him. He communicated mainly by sighs and weary movements of his hand.

Then there was the General, a great-uncle, I believe. He was an aged, frail, and saintly Iranian Father Zossima, having now become, at the end of his life, a mystic. He had had, however, a terrible past, famous for the number of men he had ruined and for his incessant wenching. He had also been a maniacal hunter, and there was the story told by someone who, visiting his country house, had seen the carcasses of twenty newly killed gazelles laid out on the terrace. But all this was in the past. Now, as he once told me, he put sugar out for the mice in his house. As for the wenching, when his kinsmen's conversation became off-color, as it so very often did, he would turn away to give pious attention to his prayer beads.

These descriptions may suggest that all of the Prince's kinsmen were preposterous. This was not the case. There were others who were quite ordinary, and not particularly interesting. An exception to both categories, the preposterous and the dull, was the Prince's only full brother, an intelligent and charming man, a great sportsman, and one of the more respected members of the Iranian parliament.

Kinswomen were often also present, usually one or the other of the Prince's stepmothers. The old Prince-Governor had had the four wives allowed by Shiah Islam plus a number of concubines. The Prince's mother was dead, but the three stepmothers survived and the Prince — not always the case in such a situation — was fond of all of them. There was one in particular who visited regularly and whom I liked very much. She would sit by the brazier smoking opium, a tiny woman right from a Persian miniature: the little heart-shaped face, red cheeks, jet black page-boy hair, perfect eyebrows. There were almost always tears in her eyes and she was almost always smiling.

The Prince's visits to this sitting room usually resulted in fun or a fight. When the fun was on, it normally consisted of hilarious, outrageous gossip about some member of the family not present. A simple, innocuous happening would be exaggerated and colored up until all of them were rolling on the floor, including the "fat thing" in the corner, and even the cousin with the mandarin manners. One evening the Prince told the story of a girl of the family who had recently married. The poor girl had suffered all her life — or at any rate was so accused — from severe flatulence. On the night of her marriage, the Prince reported (or invented), her parents, hoping to disguise this weakness at least on her wedding night, had subjected the girl to a funnel and a half bottle of cologne. Later in the evening, while the marriage was being consummated, the bridegroom was said to have complained to his bride of a strange odor, "half sweet, half sour." The bride, it was alleged, had replied, "Do you, sir, not recognize the fragrance of a Qajar princess?"

So the jokes and tales went on, everyone getting it, the Prince as well when he was absent. As for the fights, I always withdrew before they had time to reach full strength, but from the screaming, bellowing, and thumping that came from the sitting room, they must have been very violent.

The sitting room of the riffraff was also a lively place. Here the Arab, the Prince's "friend" was often to be found, and it was also the hangout of the Mouse and the Monster. Another regular was a local carpenter, a master at his craft and a famous debauchee. There was, too, a taxi driver-cum-pimp, a teahouse keeper, and a well-known local gambler. As in the kinsmen's sitting room, there was much friendliness as well as fighting. The camaraderie took several forms. One was a great deal of friendly cursing: "You donkey's cunt . . . whore's bastard . . . mother fucker . . . ," and for good measure, "sister fucker" and "brother fucker."

The camaraderie also took the form of the pledges of loyalty and subservience exchanged among Iranian men of this class. The most common are "Your servant" and "Your slave," but there are others as colorful as the curses. "I am the piss of your beer . . . the dust beneath your feet . . . the louse on your body. . . ." The sitting room constantly resounded with these curses and pledges.

The two most common activities in this sitting room, not counting the drinking, were dancing and dicing. The

dance was the usual Iranian solo belly dance, which in
Iran is performed as often by men as by women — in fact
by everybody, even children and the old. The riffraff
had their own form of it, the hat well down over one eye
and in the hand of the extended arm a flower or, if that
was lacking, a handkerchief. The bumps and grinds were
pronounced.

The dicing was conducted in a very spatty fashion,
mainly because there was so much cheating. Iranians are
profoundly bored by rules, the rules of games, the rules
of government, and even — so at least a Sunni Moslem
would say — the rules of religion. In any event, there was
often a great deal of slippery dice work, and it was this
that often caused the fights.

Even when the other entertainment rings were going
full blast, the Prince would get to the riffraff more often
than to the rest. For one thing, they were among his favorite guests and, for another, it was here that he could,
without curiosity from the foreigners or possible disap-
proval by the kinsmen, take a long swig of *shireh.* Not
long after I met the Prince, he had had to give up smoking opium since the bullet was giving his lungs more
trouble. *Shireh* is a liquid form of opium. He drank it
mixed with vodka, a potent combination.

So the Prince would come, fresh perhaps from the foreigners and a discussion of Sartre or the Cento Plan, to sit
with his riffraff, swigging the *shireh,* clapping out a beat
for them to dance to, settling, or trying to, the dicing
fights. He had, as I have said, a particular affection for
these men. And it was, I think, because they had spirit,
held certain old-fashioned ideas concerning loyalty in
friendship, and believed in enjoying the flesh — one of
the better ways to lead a life, he probably thought.

The sitting room where the foreign guests gathered

was, compared to the others, a rather formal room. There were chairs and sofas around — elsewhere in the house one sat on carpets. There was, too, a large oil painting of the Prince-Governor over the fireplace, all eyes and moustache and posed against a gloomy Watteau landscape. (The Prince-Governor had died at ninety-two. "Thrown from his horse," was the usual explanation given to the foreign guests, though the Prince once confessed to me that in fact the old man had died in a fall from his toilet seat.) And finally, swinging from the ceiling, overpowering everything, was a large, not very good crystal chandelier.

All kinds of people gathered to sit beneath the threatening chandelier: the young in their beads and feathers en route to Katmandu, American widows on Swan tours, archaeologists and anthropologists — the latter as common in Iran then as the lice used to be — ambassadors, university professors, and corporation chairmen. The Prince offered his hospitality to all of them, equally agreeable to the gauche youth and the urbane ambassador. They all found him wonderfully informed about Iran and able to impart that information with lucidity and charm. Unlike many Iranians, he was not ashamed of his country's ordinary, traditional life. He was among the first to value — all the fashion now — its crafts and folkways. This made him especially interesting to the foreigners, for these were their interests, too. Most of them had not come to Iran to see industrial parks and the new bad architecture; they had seen enough of both at home. On the other hand, the Prince was proud of Iran's material development. He knew enough about the old days to be glad that the new building, however atrocious its architecture, housed a hospital. In fact he was impatient and so sometimes sarcastic about the pace of this development.

Once a servant brought in a bag of potato chips. They had only recently appeared on the market and were not very good. "We wish to manufacture motorcars," he said, "and yet we cannot even make potato chips."

The thing, however, that I think most foreigners remembered from their time beneath the chandelier was simply the generosity and grace of the Prince's hospitality. He made everyone feel that he, the Prince, was especially happy to have him in his house. There was, in particular, his unfailing special attention to those who were ill at ease, his quickness to anticipate a need, from a pillow for some old woman to a hot bath for some weary archaeologist. However, there was another side to this which some might call a failing. Though the Prince was ready to go to great trouble for his guests, he expected his guests to remember that he had gone to the trouble. In short, he believed in the old custom of the bread-and-butter letter. He did not always get them and some of those he got he did not consider adequate. He once took a foreign consul on a ten-day tour of tribal country and did it very grandly: a hamper of champagne, iced caviar, the other luxury touches. In return for this he received a rifle which he described as "hardly better than a BB gun."

Though the Prince did not ordinarily mix people, now and then it happened that there would be a group of guests who, though very different from each other, nonetheless, and by some unknown law, blended well together. When this was the case, the Prince did not hesitate to mix them.

For some reason or other, these gatherings usually took place in the courtyard, perhaps the most agreeable place in the Prince's house. Iranian courtyards seldom depart from a certain plan: a pool in the middle at which four paths meet, the paths forming four squares filled with small trees and flowers. The Prince's courtyard followed this plan, but to the basic form he had added much.

Over the whole area there was a high cat's cradle of ropes — a kind of visual booby trap — twined with morning glories. The periphery of the court was planted with miniature cypress and pine, sunflowers at random in among these, and Jack-and-the-beanstalk plantings of corn.

One of the pleasantest things about the courtyard was the kitchens, two, big, beam-ceilinged rooms which opened on to its farthest end. There was always much going on in the kitchens: the cooking, the wild card games and squabbling of the Mouse and the factotums, Sultaneh calmly going about her work of pickling, juicing, and jam making. Some of the kitchen work was done outside: trays of greens and rice to be washed, a press with a pile of pomegranates beside it, Sultaneh working a mortar and pestle, the great steaming copper cauldrons. There was almost always the fragrance of wood smoke and the smells of cooking food in the courtyard.

The place where our mixed gatherings occurred was a flagged area at the end of the courtyard opposite the kitchens. It was like a terrace, facing the pool, a facade of niched French doors bowered in jasmine at the rear of it. Here the Prince would set out some canvas chairs, a few low tables — originally used as stands for water pipes — a butler's tray of vodka and fruit juices, a tub of ice. For those who preferred the ground there was a rattan mat and pillows.

I remember the courtyard best the summer Madame Pagent — the woman who introduced me to the Prince — was staying at the house, for she and the Prince were old friends. She would totter down at about six-thirty, a glass of vodka in her hand, perfumed and painted, dressed like an expensive woman. In her youth, and well into middle age, she had been a beauty, but she was not a foolish woman and now, in her sixties, she was not attempting to look thirty. Nonetheless, she had decided to keep what she had as well as she could, and indeed there was in that carefully cared-for, fragile, fading perfection much that was pleasing and very gallant.

When Madame Pagent arrived, the Prince would go to her in the doorway where she waited for him and take her hand, complimenting her on how well she looked, and then lead her to a chair to sit among the others, all of whom would rise and bow, as men had always done for her. She in turn would lean forward to each, inquiring of his health and then settle back to drink her vodka.

The others there usually included the mandarin-mannered cousin, the clown, Hassan, and several members of the riffraff. Among the latter there was Akbar Da'i, the teahouse keeper, a short, Buddha-faced little man who engaged in much sighing and raising of his eyes to heaven. Whenever he drank, which was often, he would politely lean toward us and propose some elaborate, old-fashioned toast, drain the glass, and then, like a prissy old woman, carefully wipe his lips. The carpenter often showed up as well, sometimes bringing with him his apprentice, a pimply, crow-shouldered little boy with happy, expectant eyes, who would sit there, never speaking, watching us. The Arab of course was present, but his rival that summer, a young gendarme, would sometimes be there too. Finally, my friend Jahan Shah dropped in now and then, for he and the Prince were old cronies. He still had not found Fatima a husband, and he would try each time he came to induce the carpenter to take her as a second wife.

So we would sit around, some in chairs, the riffraff and

the clown on the rattan mat, some sipping vodka, others puffing opium, all of us watching the dusk come down. The Prince, more often than not, would slowly pace the terrace, stopping occasionally to enter the conversation. His costume on these courtyard evenings could be bizarre. I remember him once in red knickers, tennis shoes, a blue jersey, and over all of this a homespun tribal alb. Another time he had on the black wide-legged peasant trousers topped incongruously by a white golf cap. It was almost as if he wore these outlandish combinations — and there were many others — in order to entertain us, and perhaps, too, because he believed that life should be more a costume party than it is.

It always struck me as wonderful that our conversations in the courtyard went along as well as they did. After all, we each spoke out of such different experiences. Still, somehow, things fitted together. The cousin, for example, might get on to his memories of England and George V, thus provoking from Akbar Da'i, the teahouse keeper, a question concerning George's moustache — was it strong and ample as befitting a king? Or Madame Pagent might remark on a fine piece of crystal she had seen in a shop, and the carpenter would then observe that glass was a dead material and, unlike his wood, capable only of breaking, never of mellowing. No subject, however abstruse, ever left the riffraff, or anybody else for that matter, at a loss for a comment. One evening the Prince made some reference to the theater of the absurd, describing some of its characteristics. "Rather like our evenings," Madame Pagent said with her rich vodka laugh. "I shall apply for a part," said the clown. "Theater of life might be a better name for it," suggested the carpenter. "The West is mad," pronounced Jahan Shah. Such were some of my times at the Prince's house.

There remains another, however, the most vivid of them all. One Christmas Eve, some friends in the town had asked me to take dinner with them. Finding myself in town a little early, I decided to make a brief call on the Prince. It was the coldest night I had ever known in Iran. The square in front of the Prince's house was completely deserted. Even mad Zareh, a vermin-ridden old beggar woman who made the square her hangout, was gone.

Ebrahim let me into the Prince's house. I went up to the second floor, hearing music as I went. At the door of the large sitting room I stopped, unable to believe my eyes. The Prince was waltzing down the room with Zareh the beggar woman. On the table were a platter of chicken bones and a half bottle of Hennessy's.

"What are you doing?" I said, reprovingly.

"Merry Christmas," the Prince called back to me.

"What on earth are you doing?" I asked again. He led the old woman to a chair.

"The poor old thing," he said. "She has no friend, no one cares for her." Then he turned toward the window, his head thrusting as though he were sniffing at the coldness and the falling snow. "And it is such a bitter night."

It was perhaps the deepest act of charity I had ever seen — done by this Moslem prince on Christmas Eve.

Why it was I do not quite know, but during the later years of my friendship with the Prince, it was more often at his village that I saw him. To get there one passed through some of the most beautiful country in our district, a series of deep valleys, green with plane and poplar, checked buff with village houses. All around soared the

mountains, their summits peat brown and streaked with
snow, their lower slopes pastel-colored as the barren
mountain slopes of Iran are — pink, pale blue, apricot,
and green.

The last of these valleys was Samonzar. Coming down
from the pass one saw it below, boat-shaped, about five
miles long, wheat and clover growing in it. At the far end
stood the village in clumps of green against the foothills,
the pitched metal roofs of the Prince's manor house dor-
mering the green like a scattering of treehouses.

The manor house stood at the outskirts of the village
facing a half-moon of poplars and a big lobed pool filled
with scummy water. It looked like something built by a
Milwaukee beer baron at the turn of the century, not a
beautiful house but impressive and remarkable for being
there in the wilds of Iran.

Built of the usual plastered-over mud, it was a square,
tall structure with two stories of sagging verandas around
three sides and a short gabled portico projecting from the
front. Some of the pillars of the porch had fallen, their
sections lying in the grass. The doorway was a black maw,
its great walnut doors, carved with wheat sheaves, permanently swung back.

Inside it was too dim to make out much: a big hall, its
limits lost in shadows, double doors half-open into rooms
empty except for litter. At the back, through an arch,
rose the stairway. The stone of the steps, cut from a riverbed, bore watermarks, as though the water still lapped
over it. Whenever someone climbed the stairs, the creak-
ing banisters would disturb the birds nesting on the cornices above, and they would swoop about in the upper
dimness and around the black chain from which, in the
old days, a massive chandelier had hung.

On the second floor there was only one room in use and

it was used rarely. This was the petit salon. Above the wainscoting there was a tapestry wallpaper of silvery chrysanthemums on a cream ground — in shreds. The ceiling was mottled with damp as was the molded plaster of the Empire fireplace. Around the room stood slipper chairs in stained yellow satin. Yet for all its shabbiness, it was a pleasant room, especially when the sun came slanting in, for the time gilding it again. There were still a few touches of the old elegance: two bronze goddesses on the mantelpiece; and on a table in the center of the room, a big crystal pitcher held in a webbing of chased silver — a gift to the Prince-Governor from the last czar — into which the Prince, when he had guests, would put a big bouquet of flowers, often the yellow irises which so abounded at Samonzar and which gave the room the smell of lemons.

This was the room used by the Prince when he had important guests. If there were too many for the slipper chairs, carpets and bolsters were put down, the bolsters improvised from saddlebags stuffed with hay. There were often such reminders at Samonzar that one was deep in the country. I remember one afternoon when the Prince served martinis to his guests. There being no ice, no electricity to make it, each guest received his glass bedded in a bowl of snow which had been brought down donkey-back that morning from the mountains.

There was only one other inhabitable room in the house. (The Prince sometimes called his house "Alipolis," a pun he had made from his first name, Ali, and the suffix of the famous ruin Persepolis.) This was the gun room, a small, snug place overflowing with a mad variety of objects. Tinned food and K rations were stacked everywhere as if siege or a long winter were expected. On a shelf above the door stood a glass jar of frankincense.

The bookcase contained Toynbee, Maugham, *The Boston Cook Book,* Tolstoy's mystical works, *Reader's Digest.* Against one wall there was a Victorian commode, Pear's soap in the soap dish, and next to it leaned a pair of riding boots filled, for some unknown reason, with grain. From hooks around the room hung such things as a nurse's red-lined cloak, an old-fashioned hand-seeder, a fisherman's hat brought back from Capri, hanks of uncarded wool, and an enormous fly swatter. China vases and mason jars were set about the room and filled with fading wildflowers and the yellow irises. Photos hung everywhere: a gallery of family portraits, the Spanish Steps, a tea party on a Thames launch, a Rhenish castle, and two oleographs, one of the Prophet, the other of Hezrat-e-Ali. Even the floor was cluttered. Except for a space in the center for the brazier, it was covered with upholstered mattresses and pillows.

On the wall by the door hung the gun rack; it held pistols, revolvers, Mauser rifles, and several antique guns, their stocks inlaid with mother-of-pearl, verses from the Koran chased on their barrels. On another wall there was a saddlecloth of claret-colored Kashan velvet. A long curved sword rested on prongs at its center. Below the cloth, like a kind of fringe, twelve knives hung vertically, their blades engraved with arabesques, their hilts of bone or ivory, some inlaid with rings of turquoise.

The gun room's one French door opened onto a small farm garden with hollyhocks, stocks, and lilacs in rough beds to either side of the door — the beds fenced with split rails to keep stray cattle out. The door had a fine sill, a thick, smooth slab of that riverbed rock, and it was a good place to sit in the morning in the sun and watch the peasants going by with their donkeys, nets of clover or hay slung across the donkeys' backs, or the grooms — for the stables were on this side — walking the horses in the grove that lay beyond the garden.

At night, too, the gun room was a pleasant place to be: the curtains drawn, the lamps lit, coals glowing in the brazier, and the tall glass chimneys of the lamps, like so many little convex mirrors, reflecting and multiplying in miniature the profusion of the room — the seeder, the boots, the hanging knives, the jar of frankincense.

My visits to Samonzar rarely lasted more than several days. The principal entertainment, aside from reading and walking, was the Prince himself, in particular watching him deal with his peasants. The relationship was a paternal one: a cranky, generous, slightly mad father with children who were, in almost every case, incorrigible and up to mischief. At least half of every day was taken up with exchanges between them. The peasants would stand outside the gun room door, waiting respectfully to be received by the Prince — though when his back was turned there would be much wiggling, winking, and grinning at his expense.

Often these calls were for medical attention. This was ordinarily given in the form of pills, any kind of pills which happened to be at hand. Once the Prince, either absent-mindedly or because he was fed up with the constant calls on his attention, doled out sleeping tablets in great numbers. By afternoon almost the entire village was sound asleep.

Many of the calls too were for the purpose of complaint — the inevitable, interminable complaints over the working out of the agricultural shares. The old Iranian arrangement between landlord and peasant was based on a share-crop system, the landlord usually contributing the land, water, and seed in return for a certain share of the crop. The amount of this share was the source of much bickering and duplicity on the part of everyone concerned.

So, for example, a peasant would call and, after much complimenting of the Prince on his generosity and other beating around the bush, would make his claim for a greater share. The Prince, meanwhile, would stride about the room, striking poses, eating peanuts, rubbing his face with hand lotion, alternately praising the peasant and reminding him of his bad ways, broken promises, and laziness. The peasant in turn would remind the Prince that he, the peasant, had eight children and further that he, his father, his father's father, and so on, had always been the Prince's faithful slaves. These generations of "faithful" service, it was implied, should be borne in mind. It all reminded me very much of the night I had watched Jahan Shah dealing with his peasants.

Rarely in these very Iranian conversations was there any mention of the relevant facts, relevant, that is, to the Western mind — how much land and water the Prince had provided, how much fertilizer and labor had been provided by the peasant. What was of importance here was the position of the two men and the relationship between them. Who knows, perhaps the peasant's mother had been wet nurse to the Prince's favorite brother. It is things such as these that are the "facts" in many Iranian dealings.

The discussions between the Prince and his peasants were often prolonged, and one reason for this was that they were often interrupted by the Prince so that he might give vent to some impulse. Once I saw him break off a discussion to put on the Capri hat, take the hand-seeder, and there, beyond the hollyhocks, nodding in the great hat, begin to sow clover. He did this because he felt like doing it and also, perhaps, to give his peasants an example of "industry," though if they had known about it they would, I think, have thought rather of Marie Antoinette in her dairy.

Another time he amazed me — but not the peasants, who had seen everything — by coming back into the room after a brief absence wearing a Riviera bikini, the nurse's cloak on his shoulders, and holding a large towel lettered "The Ritz." He wished to take a splash in the pool before continuing what had seemed to me a rather urgent conversation. I often wondered how his peasants took these bizarre interludes. I suppose they accepted them much as people in some little feudal state would have accepted, and grown used to, the ways of a mad but good-hearted king.

In addition to the peasants, there was at Samonzar another group of persons, and these, as I learned more about them, helped to explain a look that sometimes came into the Prince's face — the look that one sees on a man for whom life in some important way has not worked out. These persons were the Prince's "children."

First there was his "son," Sohrab. He was in his twenties when I used to go to Samonzar — a husky, bowlegged little fellow, gruff and heavy. According to the Prince, Sohrab had made his first appearance when he was about a month old, wrapped in a rag, his stomach swollen, found literally on the Prince's doorstep. The Prince had taken him in and sent for Sultaneh, the old nurse, to come and care for him. The Prince loved to tell the story of how, when the child was a little older, he, the Prince, would take Sohrab to the petit salon and stand him on the mantelpiece between the two bronze ladies, whose height he was then, and of how the child would embrace one or the other of the ladies and smile down at him.

It was, I think, one of the best memories the Prince had

of Sohrab, for this son had not turned out well. When I knew him, he appeared to have no duties, no job, and no interests, though he liked fooling about with the Prince's horses and did a little training. The Prince always treated him with a kind of sad deference, as if puzzled by this gift which God had given him but which had become of so little account.

Then there was his "daughter," Mitra. She had been found in a tree at the back gates of the manor house. As in the case of Sohrab, the Prince had raised her and, since she had shown more promise, had sent her when she was eight to a convent of French nuns in Isfahan. There she learned French and English, embroidery, and deport-ment, and became, in short, a little lady. He had, I am sure, flamboyant plans for her — a time in Paris; a posi-tion as lady-in-waiting, perhaps, to his cousin, who was then queen; a great marriage. But when she was sixteen, spending a part of her summer holidays at the village, she fell in love with a village boy. The Prince threatened de-struction to herself and to the whole village and sent her away. But she came back and married the boy, and when I was at Samonzar she lived there in a simple farmhouse, the English and French long forgotten, a plain village woman. The Prince always called on her at Iranian New Year and in general kept an eye on her — there was, pa-thetically, an unused piano in the farmhouse, once sent by the Prince. But he never mentioned her, which showed his hurt.

Finally, there was Abbas, not referred to as his "son" but rather as "my one-time protégé" — for he too had been a failure. It seemed that one afternoon, some years before, the Prince had been sitting by the gun room door when a widow of the village passed by with her boy, the boy all splattered with mud and bleeding. The Prince called to the woman and asked her what had happened. The boy had been in a fight with some other peasants over water (a frequent cause of bloodshed and even death in Iran) and they had beaten him badly with their hoes. The Prince took the boy in, washed his wounds and bound him up, and then, out of both pity and liking for the lad, told him that if he wanted he could have a job in the kitchens of the manor house. The boy, though his job was only dishwasher, showed remarkable talent for cooking, and so after a time the Prince sent him to the town and apprenticed him to a famous cook. The cook, instead of teaching him to cook, taught him to whore, drink, and gamble, and in time Abbas became a debauchee. At some point the Prince got wind of this and summoned the cook and Abbas to his town house. He punched them both in the face and then sent Abbas back to Samonzar where, in my time, he was cook, when sober. "The fool," the Prince once said, after Abbas had served us a fine soufflé, "if he had behaved himself, he might now have been at one of our embassies, perhaps even with the royal family." He said it with anger but also sorrow, for that look came into his eyes and perhaps he was thinking, too, of his other "children." For he, a man who liked to give, could have given most to them, and yet here he had been stopped.

Of all my visits to the Prince at Samonzar, the one I remember best was the last. I arrived at night, tired and covered with dust. The Prince told me to go to the hall and bathe. The servants brought lamps, a tub, pitchers of hot water, shampoo, and towels. One of them poured the water and shampooed my hair; another brought a change of clothes — a pair of peasant trousers and a shirt, warmed at the brazier. I put these on and went out to the Prince, who was sitting on a carpet on the veranda. A

Drambuie frappé was waiting for me on a silver tray.

Some of the men from the village were on the veranda as well, sitting back on their knees in a semicircle around the Prince. Among them was Kamal Khan, the man who some years before had shot the Prince and was now his chief agent at the village. It seemed a strange thing to me, this forgiveness, though I was well aware that for the Prince, as for any Iranian, evil was known to be in every man and could not be held against him, any more than winter might be held against the year or darkness blamed for following the day.

They talked for a while about village matters: a marriage that was coming up, some feud, a water reservoir to be repaired. Then the Prince called for the meat which we were to have for supper. It was brought, a fine hunk of it on a wooden board, and also pots of salt and pepper and a tray of herbs. The Prince set to work, rubbing the herbs and the other things into it, patting it all over when he had finished. Another tray was brought with string and a scissors, and with these the Prince neatly and securely bound the meat into a kind of loaf. He tossed it once in the air, then gave it to the cook to roast.

While the Prince had been preparing the meat, others had come up to join the circle: Sohrab, a saddle on his lap, oiling it; the clown, sleepy with hashish; and some villagers, including two women. The Prince appeared very glad to see the women, and he and they began to joke and chaff one another. They sat cross-legged in front of him, their veils falling cloaklike from their heads, their faces strong like those of gypsy women. Only their hands, coarse and thick from work, lay still, as though tired, in their laps. Laughing, they would sway into each other, heads touching, and in their rich country Iranian hoarsely whisper jibes at the Prince. He would then slap his knee in pleasure at this liberty they were taking with him. "Pedar sag," he would give them back — "your father is a dog" — that Iranian phrase which can serve for either affection or abuse, in this case, as was obvious, for affection.

This intimacy between the peasant women and the Prince surprised me. He must have guessed this, for after bantering on a little longer with them, he turned and explained that they were his milk sisters, the daughters of his wet nurse, and so there was a special bond between them. This led him to the subject of his childhood and the system according to which he had been raised.

He, and boys like him, he explained, stayed with a wet nurse until they were about three and then, weaned, they were given over to what he called a trainer. His trainer, apparently not uncommonly, was a milk brother. The job of the trainer was to teach the boy how to wash and dress himself, how to act before his elders, and then, a little later, how to ride and shoot. Also, the trainer gave simple lessons in natural science, the names and movements of the stars, and something on the local animals and plants. When the time came, and it comes early in Iran, the trainer would teach the boy about women, the gallantries and forms of respect due to them but also some detailed information on the methods of lovemaking.

The Prince also had another teacher, in addition to the trainer, and this had been an elderly and learned Sufi. His function was to instruct the Prince in the Koran and in the mystical poets of Iran. Finally — and this in the old days had been a customary feature of aristocratic education — he had been taught a trade, shoemaking in his case. I knew that the Prince mended his own shoes, but I had assumed that this was simply an eccentricity on his part. It did not occur to me that it might be a normal ac-

complishment for an Iranian prince, yet it is perfectly un-
derstandable when one reflects on the turmoil of Iran's
three thousand years of history, at so many points of
which a prince one day might be a pauper the next.

That, then, had been the Prince's education until he
was sent to England. It explained much to me: his rough
familiarity with the peasant women, the expert way he
had trussed up the roast, his way with animals, the things
he could brew from plants, his manner of entering a
room. Taken all together, it explained that special grace
of his, the grace that comes from balance.

Time passed and finally the roast was ready, everyone
staying on for dinner. When we had finished, I complimented him on the roast and also on the Drambuie frappés, telling him the frappés were the best I had had since
Harry's Bar in Venice, a place he knew. "Harry's Bar,"
he said, his head down. "I wonder. Where should we
be? Here or there?" Then he looked up, his head making the circuit of the figures around us — Kamal Khan,
the women, the sleeping clown, Sohrab. "Ah, surely
here," he said.

The next day was typical of our days at Samonzar. We
washed and shaved in the sun of the gun room garden
and then went in to a breakfast of tea, curds, and bread.
After breakfast the Prince began his usual interviews,
while I went off to the orchard to read. That day, as we
often did, we took our lunch there on a carpet. Then,
after a rest, we went to pay a visit to the stables.

The Prince kept about twenty horses. He did nothing
with them. As far as I could tell he simply kept the animals out of fondness, though he may also have held the
idea that a Prince should have many horses.

These visits to the stables were rather formal. The
head groom would meet us at the doorway and, bowing,

wave us in. He was a watery-eyed old fellow with a peg leg and a phlegmy voice, dressed always in an old, brass-buttoned, green coat. The horses were his life. I once came across him in the grove, his arm around the neck of an Arab mare, his cheek brushing her forelock, muttering, "my darling, my darling."

Late that afternoon I went for a walk in the valley — a walk I always took at Samonzar. The valley was a place of extraordinary beauty. The colored mountain slopes drew back and up from it as if to show the perfection they guarded: the long, green pool of wheat, the silver strokings of the poplar groves, the inlets between the lower slopes where the orchards lay, in spring blotting the edges of the valley pink. Part of the valley's beauty came, too, from its curious but satisfying contrasts: that perfect flatness in the midst of raging mountain peaks, the utter silence of the place made now and then profounder by sounds — the calls to prayer, a yodeled greeting, herd bells — all striking in the silence with a gentle clarity like clock chimes in a house at night. There was, too, the valley's seeming emptiness, as if man had not yet found it. In fact, however, I never walked there without encountering someone: a peasant spading a water channel, women with baskets on their heads far out in the wheat, herdsmen bringing their cattle home for the night. Yet still there was that sense of emptiness. It may have been that the people lived in the valley in awe and humbleness, so their presence barely touched it, and it seemed that there was only the valley itself.

That afternoon I followed one of the water channels, for the wheat was high and it was difficult to go cross-country in it. I went along some distance, listening to the silence and watching the sky, which had begun to flare a little in the west with the approaching sunset. There was no movement in the valley, only the wheat leaning in the light wind then coming on with evening. Suddenly, into the middle of this, thrashing through the wheat, came the Monster, the gentleman's gentleman, the Prince's old valet.

It had been several years since he had held that post and, for that matter, since I had last seen him. At some point the Prince had sent him back to the village as his "secret agent." This arrangement had not worked out well for anyone. The peasants took to bribing the Monster with chickens and other things in return for the withholding of information from the Prince. For a time the Monster had ridden high, but eventually the Prince caught on and he was dismissed. Now, he told me, as we walked together toward the manor house, he was in terrible straits, so poor, no work; worst of all, he was not trusted by anyone, neither the peasants nor the Prince. I felt sorry for him, the poor half-stupid boy, his great head, as we walked along, swinging like that of some animal that had been struck. I told him I would speak to the Prince — wanting to, and knowing as well that he would have asked me to intercede at some point anyway. He thanked me and said that in the morning he would go to the village shrine and light a candle in gratitude for my act.

I looked up at the shrine — for it lay to the right of us, crowning one of the nearer hills — a small, square, mud building with a dome in black and yellow tile, shaped like a tulip. The local people believed that the nurse of Fatima, the Prophet's daughter, was buried there. I knew, too, that the graves of the Prince's mother and favorite brother were there as well. By now the dome of the shrine was the last thing in the valley to hold the light, a flame there against the darkening shoulders of the mountains. This last light was the sign for the evening call to prayer, which began then as we came to the end of our walk, the long, intoned affirmation of God's being, reaching us there in the valley like a great horn played high in the mountains.

I left the Monster at the door of the manor house and went in to find everyone gathered in the gun room. It was too cold that night for the veranda. But not so cold that they had not left open the door of the gun room in order to see the new moon rise. Now and then puffs of cool, woody air came into the room and the Prince would raise his head from his book and take in deep breaths of it. The clown was there, carving a doll for one of his grandchildren, and Sohrab too, staring into space. I sat down, saying nothing, not wanting to break the silence.

A little later we took dinner and afterwards sat on talking, the Prince being in a story-telling mood. Some mention of a wolf that had attacked a flock of sheep the night before reminded him of a winter some years past, when a wolf had come to the house itself. It was, he said, the coldest winter they had ever had at Samonzar, and he, his secretary Aqa Ahmad, and the old nurse Sultaneh had been confined to the manor house for nearly a week. One night all three were in the gun room telling stories when they heard a great thump and the sound of breaking glass. Taking lamps, they ran into the hall, where the noise had come from, and there they saw it: the forepaw of a wolf thrust through the broken transom, the paw down, clawing at the inside of the door. Apparently the snow had drifted in under the portico and the wolf was standing on the drift trying to get into the house, where he sensed that there was warmth. The Prince ran back to the gun room and grabbed the sword that hung on the Kashan saddlecloth. With this he slashed off the wolf's paw and the animal went howling off into the night.

When the Prince finished the story he was frowning, explaining that he had never felt quite right about this act. Wolves, there was no doubt, were the villagers' greatest enemy — after landlords, he added, laughing — but on the other hand this wolf, because of the terrible coldness of the night, was seeking shelter and thus. . . . It was clear that the incident remained a dilemma in his mind and this did not surprise me, for traditional Iranian ideas of hospitality, of a stranger in need, even if the stranger be an animal, go very far indeed.

His mention of the sword prompted me to ask him whether, as I had assumed, it had a place of honor there because it had belonged to some brave ancestor. He answered no, that it was not hung there to remind him of bravery but rather as a reminder of how untoward a man's actions could be. The sword, he explained, had belonged to his "seventh ancestor," Abul Hussain, a man famous for his goodness and courage. One night Abul Hussain, while on campaign, was sleeping in a cave. In the middle of the night he got up to make water. At the mouth of the cave, knowing it possible that enemies might be lying there in wait for him, he slashed the darkness with his sword, in one stroke cutting off the head of his most faithful servant, who had been standing guard there to protect him. "How often," he said quietly, "I have done that in my way."

During the talk and tales I had been vaguely aware, from the corner of my eye, of some movement beyond the gun door. Now, as we sat silently thinking of the Prince's story, I tried to make out what it was. Then I saw it again and the bulk of the Monster suddenly profiled in the moonlight. This reminded me of my promise, and so I began to introduce the subject to the Prince, in the Ira-

nian way: how all men are venal, even the best, that all
make mistakes, even the seventh ancestor. Then, when
all this had been agreed to, I mentioned the Monster.
"Ha," said the Prince, seeing the trap. He turned and
with narrowed eyes looked out at the figure waiting in the
moonlight. He motioned him in and the Monster came,
standing by the door, his great head down on his breast,
his fingers twisting and trembling together.

"You know," the Prince said to me in English, "we have
an expression in Iranian. We say that a man given intelligence may — and indeed more often than not will —
become a 'thief with a lamp'. This thief," he motioned
toward the Monster, "not only has no lamp but is blind as
well. He would do better to change his profession." He
said no more and took up his book.

Iranians, as I have said, seem to me more forgiving
than many people, but, like anyone, they like it made easy,
for the humbleness it requires is hard for them as well.
So "Do it for me," I said to the Prince. He continued to
look at the book, but after a moment he put it down and
slowly took from his pocket some bills, which he threw at
the Monster's feet. Then he gave the boy his orders.
The next morning he was to set off for Meshed, a three-
day journey, and there at the tomb of Imam Reza do
repentance. That done, the Prince would see what could
be arranged in the way of a job.

Even before the Prince finished the Monster had begun
to sob, crawling along the floor, blubbering at the Prince's
hand. It was a hideous sight, the abasement of the poor
caught creature, and the Prince, with a look of pain and
fear on his face which I had never seen before, sharply
drew back his hand and touched for an instant the boy's
ear, saying quickly and quietly, as if trying to take back
what had happened, "No, no." Then the Monster, stum-

bling, his hands across his eyes, got up to leave the room. The Prince stopped him at the door. "Would you be so good," he said, his voice gone thin, the face still with that look of pain and now quite white, "— so good as to remember me in your prayers to Imam Reza — and to beg his mercy for me."

I left early the next morning, for I had things to attend to at the farm. They were all out on the veranda to wave me goodbye. I drove away not knowing that I would never visit the manor house again — only the shrine.

One evening, a month later, an American friend and I had an invitation to dine with the Prince at his house in town. When I went to the hotel to pick up the friend, I found that she was ill and so I stayed on with her for an hour or so, knowing that it would make no difference if I arrived at the Prince's late. When I did get there I found that he did not feel well and had already retired. This surprised me. The Prince often didn't feel well — he was having more trouble with the bullet — but this had never kept him from staying up when he was expecting guests.

The light in his room was still on, so I went in to see if he was awake. What I saw startled and then frightened me. Though he was eccentric in his dress, I had never seen anything like this: he was wearing a black turban. His face was turned toward the wall.

I went over to see if he was sleeping. He was not, but I could tell that he was deep in opium, his eyes staring and dead with it. I sat down next to him and took his hand, asking what was wrong and how he felt. He didn't answer. I realized then that he was too deep in the opium and too weak to speak; so I got up and told him that I would be there that night if he needed me.

Early the next morning I was awakened by a bumping
sound and went out to find some men coming down the
hallway with a stretcher. The doctor had called and ordered the Prince to the hospital. When they had moved
him onto the stretcher and were carrying him down the
hall, he put up his hand and the clown bent down to hear
what he wanted. Then the clown went ahead and opened
the doors of all the sitting rooms, and at each one of them
the stretcher-bearers paused while the Prince looked in.
They stopped longest on the first floor, at the archway
into the courtyard. The clown lifted the Prince's head so
that he might better look into it, and the Prince made the
Moslem gesture of farewell, putting his fingers to his forehead, lips, and heart.

Hospitals in Iran have no "visiting hours." The Iranians believe that when a man is sick, the more time his
family and friends are with him, the better. The Prince's
room at the hospital and the courtyard outside the room
were thronged with people: the riffraff in great numbers,
the family of course, the "fat thing," the General, the
mandarin-mannered cousin, the old stepmothers, and
several of the half-brothers, who had flown down from
Tehran. There was even for a brief time an Englishman
who had been told to look up the Prince and who came
along to the hospital to see how he was doing.

The riffraff and I spent most of our time in the courtyard, for the Prince was in a coma and it was hard for us
to stand in the room and watch him. It was on our second morning there that we heard the terrible sound, a
kind of bellowing, like some animal protesting its pain.
We turned to see on the veranda the Arab, sobbing, his
arms stretched out, the hands up and the fingers spread
as though he were trying to keep some heavy weight
from falling on him. We knew then that the Prince was
dead.

It was later in the afternoon that I heard from the old nurse, Sultaneh, how he had died. Coming suddenly out of the coma, he had somehow gotten on his feet and gone to stand in the center of the room. There he had bowed, calling the name of his father, and then, bowing twice again, had called the names of his mother and favorite brother. Finally, with the help of Sultaneh, he got to his knees and made the last obeisance, "Besmellah, Arrahman, Arrahim" ("Oh God, the most merciful and compassionate"). When the old woman had put him back to bed, he asked for a glass of limeade, as had always been his custom before starting on a journey. He drank it. And then he left.

In the usual way he was taken to the washers where, after being washed, he was anointed with camphor and rose water and wrapped in the white gown he had worn on his pilgrimage to Mecca. The services for the dead took place the next day in four mosques — one in the town, the other three in the different parts of the country where he was known.

In the early afternoon the cortege started out for Samonzar. Halfway, at the entrance to the district in which Samonzar lay, we stopped, for the governor of the district had come on foot to honor him and to escort the body into his domain.

We stopped again at the pass leading down to Samonzar. Some time before we reached it I was puzzled. The pass was a low U-shaped defile between two hills, and looking up at the place where it was supposed to be I could not see it. But as we drew nearer I saw what had happened; the pass was completely blocked with the peasants of Samonzar, and not only the pass but the slopes around the pass were thick with them as well — those men who had cheated him so often and whom he on occasion may have cheated too, and beaten.

There was a long wait. Finally Mamdali and I got out of the Landrover and went to see what had happened. The peasants were insisting that they be allowed to carry the coffin through the valley, threatening that they would carry the hearse itself if permission were not given. After much dispute the coffin was taken out, and then there started, as had been feared, a fight over which men were to carry it first. The crowd surged, arms grappling, the coffin itself tipping and sliding above the sea of hands, once almost turning completely over. Then there began an awful screaming. It was the Monster. And at last they let him take his place at the head of the coffin.

Near dusk we reached the manor house. There the coffin was put on trestles beneath the portico. The riff-raff, the kinsfolk, the half-brothers, the servants, his "children" — all gathered around, touching it. Next the old groom came with the horses, leading them up, one by one, all twenty of them, to the bier.

Finally we began the ascent to the shrine. A cold wind had begun to blow, whistling down the draws, mixing with the cries of the mourners. At the graveyard they put the coffin down and opened it, for in the Iranian custom the coffin is used only to transport the body. We looked down at him, the long, last look of love, and then took him up and lay him gently in his grave. It was dark by then.

Journal VII

I WENT OFF this morning to Hassanabad, a village in the foothills of the mountains, some twenty miles from here. For such a small place it has a colorful and varied reputation, famous for its smugglers, pickles, waterfall, and church.

Why, among so many other villages, it alone produces smugglers, I do not know. Perhaps it is simply that this is its tradition — boys following their fathers' trade. In any event, it is an entrepôt for camel caravans which come up by secret ways from the gulf. At Hassanabad the contraband — soap, tea, foreign cigarettes, and Indian sari cloth — is transferred from the camels to jeeps for wider distribution. Several years ago, to everyone's amusement, the villagers stole the provincial gendarme commander's personal limousine to use in this traffic. The commander, either an honest man or a dishonest one dissatisfied with the smallness of the village bribe, had, it seems, been "hurting" the villagers — as law enforcement is called in our parts — and so to tweak his tail they made off with the limousine, returning it a few days later with a note suggesting that he "stop taking the bread from our children's mouths." In fact, I doubt very much that in the common mind smuggling is considered a crime at all. The civil code, of course, forbids it, but then what is the civil code, that creation of politicians? "There is nothing in the Koran," an army colonel once said to me, "about not taking cloth from Beirut to Isfahan."

The church is a rather sad tale. Christian missionaries, both American and British, have been in Iran since about the middle of the nineteenth century. I doubt whether in all that time they have made a single real convert among adult Moslems. Until recently, however, they remained optimistic. One example of this optimism is the little church at Hassanabad. How it came to be built there, I do not know, but at any rate it thrived as long as the missionaries continued to be generous with money, jobs, and favors. In time, however, the missionaries grew tired of supporting the village, and when this happened the church lost all of its members.

As for the church today, a local Armenian is its caretaker and once a year an aged, saintly Anglican priest comes to hold a service. I am told that out of consideration for the old gentleman the villagers throng the church, later hold a picnic for him at the waterfall, and load him down with their famous pickles when he leaves.

The pickles are deservedly famous, the best I have ever eaten anywhere. The problem is that I cannot stock them at the farm for fear of slighting Khanom's efforts. On the one occasion when I ventured to, Mamdali quickly and with asperity came to her defense. "Pickles from Hassanabad!" he said. "I have had the misfortune to taste them. They are pickled in piss. Are you not satisfied with Khanom's pickles?" I have not brought up the matter again, and yet that is why I went to Hassanabad this morning, though I'm not telling Mamdali and Khanom. I want a jar to take along later this week when I go with Mr. Dadgah and Mr. Bazargan on one of our hunting jaunts.

I almost missed the turnoff to Hassanabad, for it is a fortified village, its clay walls barely discernible from the mountain slopes. As I got nearer, however, the walls and towers took on, by some trick of the light, a lavender cast, and I could make out the whole complex. It reminded me of the florid illustrations of castles in my childhood books.

There was nothing romantic, however, about the main street, a narrow, rocky crevasse with an open drain running down the middle; nor about the shop where I stopped to buy the pickles, a black and filthy cave of a place. The shopkeeper, a tall, stooped old man in a green smocklike coat, fixed his eyes on me with such force and persistence that I felt I had leeches on my face.

We haggled interminably over the one jar of pickles. They were small, I said (they were not). Not daring to contradict me, he replied that this made them all the more delicate. He then went on to say that I was getting not only the pickles but also the jar. I should hope so, I replied. But the jar, he countered, (a plain, ordinary pickle jar) had such grace of form that I would treasure it always as a vase. I pointed out its crack. So we went, back and forth. Finally, winking very slowly at me, he said that due to a secret ingredient the pickles were a powerful aphrodisiac. I thought of Mr. Dadgah, Mr. Bazargan, and myself lolling in some peaceful glade, suddenly transported into paroxysms of lust. At last I bought the pickles, paying twice their worth, congratulating myself that the old devil hadn't gotten the triple he wanted out of me.

Before starting back I decided to visit the waterfall, the only one in our district and a fine one at that. To get to it I walked along the stream that issues from it. Women, squatting on the bank, were washing clothes, beating them with stones and then wringing them into twisted hanks and piling these on big copper trays. When the trays were full, they would snap out the hanks and spread them on the tree branches. The whole grove of trees through which the stream paused was patched with the bright colors of the cloth.

The waterfall lay a few yards above this washing place, a cliff with a narrow flume in it through which the water

fell, a hundred-foot white tail of it. At the rear of the
pool there was a little niche containing a candle. This, I
suspect, is what the villagers really worship, the water.
Sometimes it seems to me that Islam was no more successful in Iran than Christianity, and in fact there is a story
about a Christian missionary who after fifty years of effort
had made only one convert. "Not to worry," said a Moslem friend, "Mohammed made none."

On my way back to the car I passed the church. It
might be a little mosque except for the cross that tops the
dome. Some children were playing on the porch. They
crowded around me and asked if I would like to go into
the church and pray. I thanked them but declined.
They then asked if I wanted to buy some pickles. I
showed them my jar. Had I seen the waterfall? Finally,
one little boy said that his father could sell me Indian tea
and English soap. I was not interested. "We have nothing else to suggest," one of them said, and then they all
went away, a little sadly, I thought.

The sheik stopped in the other day for a glass of water
and I took the opportunity to chat with him, for I like his
looks and also what I know of him. What does *sheik* mean
here? I am not sure that I am altogether certain; not a
cleric; perhaps — at least in our area — half holy man,
half magician comes closest to it. In his capacity as magician our sheik finds lost articles. Mamdali sometimes
makes use of him. The sheik looks into an old mirror
and sees there where the article is hidden. Mamdali says
the sheik sometimes makes a mistake, but on the whole
Mamdali has much faith in him or, at any rate, much liking for him.

The sheik has another occupation as well. He runs a

jitney service from his village to ours. This jitney is an old
jeep into which he succeeds in stuffing an extraordinary
number of people. The sheik and his jitney are always a
pleasant sight. He dresses in immaculate white, gown and
turban, and has a kind of Bedouin face — hooked nose,
bright eyes, and a wedge of curling beard. He drives at a
fast clip, somehow giving the impression that he is holding the reins of a high-spirited horse, and always talking
and laughing as he speeds along. His passengers wave
and holler at everyone they pass. It is as if a party were
going on inside the jeep, and in a sense I think that is the
case. Every Thursday evening, the eve of the Sabbath,
the sheik distributes, as a pious act, candies in the village
square. This, together with his perennial good humor,
makes him a great favorite.

Whenever I see the sheik the subject of conversation, at
his direction, is foreign affairs — I suppose he deems this
suitable since, after all, I am a foreigner. One morning a
few years ago he stopped to see us with a newspaper (he
does not read) containing photographs of the Kennedys
and Martin Luther King. He asked me — it was the purpose of his visit — who the assassin had been. Misunder-
standing my reply, he thought that King was the culprit.
Bringing the paper to his face, he bit out King's eyes,
swallowed them, and pronounced some long rigmarole of
a curse. Horrified by what had happened, I quickly explained that poor King had been assassinated too. This
brought from him a frenzied, futile attempt to regurgitate
the eyes plus another long rigmarole meant to nullify the
curse.

The other day when he stopped for water the talk was
again of foreign affairs. "You young nations," he said,
" — you, the Russians, the British, the Germans, the rest
of the Western bunch — should be more kind, more gentle to the old societies — ourselves, the Egyptians, the oth-

ers. After all, we have in our day given much and also have gone through centuries of pain and struggle. Now we are old and tired. Why are you not more respectful to us and more caring?" I had no answer for him. "And what," he went on, "do our neighbors do for us? The Russians only send us cold, snow, and wind, while the Arabs only send us heat."

Then he was on his way, thanking us for the water, asking if we had any lost articles to be found. We watched him off down the lane, and again it seemed to me that he drove the old heap as if it were a chariot.

It looks as if the days of the mill are numbered. This morning, when I was riding by, the miller hailed me. "Look what has happened to me," he called, " — this catastrophe." I looked and saw that he was brown instead of white. The mill has been degraded to grinding turmeric.

"Come," he said, "come and share my pipe and comfort me." I tied the mare and went to sit with him on the carpet under the tree. He passed me the tube of the water pipe and I took a few puffs, watching the rose petals in the pipe's glass bowl fly about in the churning water.

"Wherever I aim, my bullet hits stone," he said. "I bought this mill five years ago thinking it would be a living until I went to feed the worms. Now look what's happened!" The story came out. Fewer and fewer of the local households are baking their own bread, and as for the bakers, they find it cheaper to buy flour from the new mechanized mill in town. "In a year, two years, they'll even be grinding turmeric with their damned engines, and then where will I be?"

It saddened me to hear all this. I am fond of the mill,

squatting there in its clearing where the three lanes meet, the tower and the huddled domes around it, and that village blacksmith's tree standing by the gate. How many times I've stopped to puff on the miller's pipe. And I would miss the miller too, cranky old fellow that he is, for there is usually some truth at the bottom of his crankiness. "We are a nation of thirty million charlatans," he once said to me. "If I had influence, knew the great ones, I could march into the gendarme post itself and take twenty thousand tomans from the box, and in clear sight of everybody, and nothing would happen to me. As it is, if my eyebrow is crooked, they will send me to court and the judge will say, 'Your eyebrow is crooked; the fine is fifty tomans.' "

I sat with him awhile and tried, as he had asked, to comfort him. He could turn the mill into a teahouse, I suggested, for our area could do with one.

"Ha," he said, "and in the back room drink and opium. Whether it would pay, I doubt, for the gendarmes would eat up all my profits in the bribes they'd force from me. But one thing I would agree. It would be an act of charity to the people. What would we do in this world if it weren't for opium and drink; think of all the suicides!"

He got up, spat, and went into the mill to come back with a sack of flour riding on his shoulders.

"I've kept by a few sacks for neighbors, friends," he said. "But it's the last you'll get from here, the last." He went over to the mare and lay the sack behind the saddle. I tried to give him some money, but he said that it must be a gift. So I thanked him and told him I hoped his generosity would bring him luck. And then, with our last flour from the mill, I rode back to the farm.

The Trip for Wood

ONE OF THE ROADS that skirted the oasis went "nowhere," the local people said. In fact it ended at an isolated place called Dehkuh, "the mountain village."

It wasn't until nearly the end of my time at the Garden that I went to Dehkuh. For one thing the road was the worst in our district, no more than a track, but more importantly travel on it put one in danger of being ambushed and robbed. This was because Dehkuh was in tribal country. There were, of course, tribesmen in our area as well — the tents I visited that afternoon when my radiator went dry, the khan, Ali Mordad, who had branded his wife — but they were few in number, for our area with its villages and orchards did not have the openness the tribes like and, for that matter, need for the movement and pasturing of their flocks.

In any event, Dehkuh was in tribal country, the mountain slopes around it serving as summer range for tribes whose winter quarters were on the littoral of the Persian Gulf. Each spring the tribes would come to these cool uplands to graze their sheep and horses and to escape the terrible heat, and then in autumn when it grew cold they would return to spend a temperate winter by the gulf.

This twice-yearly migration was, and to some extent still is, the practice of many of the tribes in southern Iran — a practice that produces strength and health and independence. It is the independence that is the rub. Government in Iran, like government elsewhere, seeks to govern. But it is difficult to educate, conscript, and tax when people will not stay put but move through country where there are few settlements or roads. For these reasons there have been attempts in recent years to settle the tribes. They have often resisted, for they hold the settled life in contempt. So it used to happen that now and then villagers and others suffered reprisals from the tribes — what we called "the trouble." The trouble might be a lonely jeep on a mountain road — fair game — the occupants, though rarely harmed, stripped of everything. The trouble, too, was the death each year of a score or so of gendarmes. And sometimes the trouble, or at any rate the cause of it, was the execution of a khan in the courtyard of our local prison.

All told, then, there was enough reason not to go to Dehkuh — that is, until we had the problem of the wood.

As I mentioned at the beginning of this book, after the murder of the gardener's boy by the son of Salar Jang, the Garden was taken over by a merchant from the town who wanted to use the place as a summer villa and so made certain renovations. He put in many windows from which to view the pool and the alley of cypress. With so much glass we had to keep a great and constant blaze in all the fireplaces in order to stay warm through the winter, so we used a lot of wood.

That last autumn at the Garden our local wood for some reason became very scarce and thus expensive, too. At about the same time I happened to hear that in the vicinity of Dehkuh there were big plantations of walnut and oak. The trouble then was less than usual, and so it seemed a good idea, in spite of the bad road, to go there and get a load of wood.

A foreigner in Iran who wants to travel deep into tribal country must get permission from the security authorities. I was given the permission, but when the officer learned that I intended to travel alone, he asked that I take a companion along, preferably someone who knew how to drive. It was desolate country, he said, not the kind of country to be alone in; also the road was worse than usual owing to heavy rains, and I would want now and then to be relieved.

Mamdali did not know how to drive, and I was not in the mood to take along any of my friends who did. I thought then of a boy who used to wash the Landrover when I went into town. He had no license, I knew, but I had seen him drive. Also, there was something in the boy I liked, his pride I think — his pride in being strong and his pride in what he implied was his high faithfulness. I liked him, too, because once, coming back to pick up the rover, I found a rose laid on the dashboard — a very Iranian thing to do, though the kind of thing that is now becoming rare. There was, finally, the practical fact that from his mother's side he was half tribesman himself. I asked him if he would like to come along, and he was ready. His name was Nemat.

We were to have started early on a Thursday morning, but owing to some problems with the pump, we were delayed until late afternoon. When, ready at last, I came out, Nemat stood holding open the door of the rover. He was wearing heavy, freshly oiled, well-made boots, twill work trousers, and a bulky knitted sweater. Looking at his big, but lanky, quick physique and his utter health — clear eyes and skin, perfect teeth, a head of thick, black, curly hair — it struck me that he would make a good companion in a fight. And it happened that, as we got into the rover, he took out from under his sweater a long knife and put it in the recess below the dashboard. "What is that for?" I asked. "I am your servant," he replied, "and I am only afraid of God." With that we started on the road to Dehkuh.

Dusk had begun to fall. The desert, faintly luminous, flowed out beyond us like the sea, on and out to the far distance where the long mountain ranges ran in jagged, inky ridges down the sky. Ahead, the road stretched straight across the desert with no end, no turn, no rise. Now and then we passed through rainpools, water splashing up in big muddy drops against the windshield. There was wind too — we could see it tousling the clumps of desert weed, and sometimes it would catch and belly out the canvas of the rover. For a time Nemat, believing it his duty to entertain me, tried to talk. But with the wind and the sound of the machine, it was impossible to hear him, and finally he gave up and began instead to sing one of those high, breaking, sad songs that Iranians love so much.

On we went, little happening, the night now around us. The road gradually became worse, especially when we reached the mountain passes, which were deeply rutted and sometimes so sharply tilted that it seemed as if the rover might topple over. At one point we passed through a village — less than a village really — a few hundred yards of high clay walls set with studded doors, shut up for the night. Some distance farther on, we saw what appeared to be a kind of wigwam tent. Then from its side a hand was raised, and we slowed down and stopped. It was a gendarme in his winter hood and cloak. He wanted a match to light a ball of desert weed, which he had gathered to make himself a fire. We gave him matches and a swallow of our vodka. He bowed to us, his hand across his heart, and we, wishing him a safe night, drove on.

The village and the gendarme, each so lonely and remote, increased our sense of isolation somehow, made it seem even more that we were on our way to nowhere. Perhaps that was why, grinding up over a ridge, we were so surprised to see Dehkuh below us, a little sprinkling of lights refracting coldly like stars in the mist of the autumn night. We drove on down, making out, as we came nearer, a building and a tower. It was the gendarme headquarters. Big men in hoods stood before the door, staring at us. Slowly, as if not quite certain, they raised their arms in greeting.

We drove on to the teahouse. It jutted out from the slope of the hill, a flat building with a long, roofed terrace, whitewashed and starkly lit. Even before I had cut the motor, Nemat was out, standing like a herald, straight and stern, pointing toward the Landrover. I was sorry then, as I seldom was, that the rover was so old and battered, for I knew that in his eyes it robbed us of dignity, that it undercut his style, as if he were playing courtier to a cross-eyed king.

Two little boys and an old man crouched on stools around a brazier in the center of the terrace. The old man stood up and offered me his stool. Nemat, with disdain, waved it aside and set up my folding chair sidewise to the brazier. Next he ordered one of the little boys to fetch the teahouse keeper, who, it seemed, was at a wedding in the village. He came almost immediately, trotting down the slope, a jaunty, youthful-looking man in a turquoise blue town shirt. Clapping his hands over the brazier to warm himself, he said that surely God had sent us, and that he was greatly honored. Then, abruptly serious, he walked to the end of the terrace, opened a timber door and, bowing, motioned us to enter.

It was a small square room with a pit in the center filled with burning coals. There were shelves high up on the walls and a ceiling of blackened tree branches. We had brought carpets from the farm, and these we spread around the pit. Then we took off our shoes and sat down tailor-fashion, our backs against the wall. It was like sitting in a flue — the blackened walls and ceiling, the smell of smoke — but snug and warm after the damp and empty night.

While I got out the vodka and Nemat fixed a little plate of goat cheese and walnuts to eat with it, the teahouse keeper talked about the snow, which would come soon and shut the village off. How, I asked, did the people keep busy through the long winter? He replied that they told each other stories and slept. Nemat, with a wink, added that there was also much time for love. The teahouse keeper turned to him as if to say, "Do not bring discredit upon this village." But Nemat went on to describe with much vividness the differences between winter love and summer love and the virtues of each — reminding me of that winter night when Jahan Shah and Fatima and I made love. Then, staring into the fire, as if seeing there what he spoke about, Nemat told us about the girl he was to marry. Like most boys of his class, he had not chosen her himself, and he would not see her until the wedding day, when together they would look into a mirror and first see each other as reflections. Yet he was sure that his mother had chosen him a fine girl because, he said, his mother loved him very much. Then he was quiet and looked again at the fire.

Into the silence came a heavy, slow knocking at the door. The teahouse keeper opened it, and we saw two tall men standing there, looking in at us. They were tribesmen. It was obvious from the kind of hat they wore — a buff-colored felt crown with a little peak at front and back. It was obvious, too, from their faces — from the long jaws and high cheekbones, and from their eyes, direct and intense, unlike the usual Iranian eyes, which are beautiful but hide something.

We stood up and asked them to come in. After an exchange of courtesies they announced the purpose of the visit. Their khan, who had heard that I was in the village, would be honored if I would call on him that night. I was surprised; the tribes, as far as I knew, had already begun their migration south. The teahouse keeper explained that the khan had been ill and was remaining in the village until strong enough to travel.

I felt like staying put and sleeping, for I had had enough of the night. On the other hand, I knew that not to go after hospitality had been offered would be to offend the tribal pride. I made the usual protests — the trouble I would give, the lateness of the hour — and then, bringing along a pint of brandy to give as a gift, we left.

Outside, the moon was just clearing the mountains above us. The mist had lifted, and the night was cold. Below us lay the village, a cluster of low domes, white and silent in the moonlight. We piled into the rover and began the descent, down a steep lane as washed out and rocky as a dry riverbed. Soon we were in the village itself, the blank, unwindowed walls rising high on either side of us. Here the lane began a series of sharp switchbacks, which led deeper and deeper down into the darkness, piling up behind us the looming jumble of the village. By now, too, we had lost the moon, and so deep were we in those ravines of high house walls that only now and then did we catch a glimpse of sky and stars. It was hard to believe that at the bottom of his maw, light and hospitality waited for us.

At an archway too narrow for the jeep to pass, we got out and began to walk down an alley, which was black and sometimes turned into short flights of crumbling steps. At last we came to the courtyard. Cypress stood like sentinels to either side of the entrance. Four paths met at a pool in the center. Opposite, beyond the pool, there was a room, arched open across the whole breadth of the court. Like the teahouse, it was whitewashed and brightly lit. Inside, a half-circle of men sat on carpets, leaning back against big bolsters, like one's idea of pashas. In the midst of them a servant knelt, fanning a brazier.

We waited on our side of the pool until we should be noticed. A man in the center of the group got up and, stepping down out of the room, came toward us, walking with a long stride, but unhurried. It was our host.

He did not introduce himself, but simply welcomed us, and then he took my hand loosely in his own and drew me along beside him. My eyes were blinded by the glare of the room, and so I couldn't see his face. I only knew that he was tall and that his voice was easy and deep. When we reached the room the men got up and bowed, and we were introduced. There was a gendarme officer — it was apparently a time of truce — a doctor from the town, and some tribesmen. We stood for a moment after the introductions, waiting for the khan to motion us to sit. He bowed and threw his hand out, as if to say that he was not deserving of our deference. But we waited until he had seated himself.

The courtesies completed, I explained the purpose of my visit to Dehkuh, that I had come to get a load of wood. The khan replied that he would put at my service some men who would show me the valley above the village, which had the best stand of walnut — a walnut, he added, that made the finest gunstocks in the world. That reminded me of something, of the time the tribes — the same tribes of which this khan was a member — had occupied the Garden and devastated it. Curious to see the khan's reaction, I mentioned in an offhand way the name of my place. I was immediately ashamed, realizing that it

had been ill-mannered of me, his guest, to have mentioned the farm, which by association brought to mind the
occupation. I felt especially bad because by now I liked
the look and feeling of the man.

There was in the long-jawed, high-cheekboned, tribal
face the tense, worn refinement of a man who had fought
hard to keep faith with himself. There was gravity, too,
though of a simple, almost humble kind. It was in the
steady strength and sadness of his eyes and in his voice,
resonant, low, and sure — the kind of voice that made
one think that with him there would always be safety. I
knew, of course, that there was another side. This is not
to say that I accuse him of deception, any more than one
would accuse a coin of guile. Simply, there was another
side which at the moment was not showing. It was the
side of ruthlessness and cruelty, though he no doubt
would have called these things discipline and punishment.
I thought of the khan who had branded his wife.

After my mention of the Garden, the khan was silent
for a moment. Then he raised his eyes and looked at me
and said that he hoped that now there was peace at the
farm and that my crops and fruit were plentiful.

With that he left me and began talking to his other
guests. From the way he turned all they said into a light
joke, it was as if he considered them absurd and yet liked
them, found them dear because of their absurdity. The
doctor, with whom he spoke the most, was a puffing,
pear-shaped man with fussy, old-fashioned manners. A
maroon silk handkerchief, drenched in some heavy scent
made from roses, spilled from his breast pocket, and he
wore a brocaded necktie, rather stained. When he smiled
or frowned — and he did much of both — his great eyebrows seemed to move halfway up and down his face. He
knew English well and told me, to my astonishment, that

205

he was fond of the works of "Miss Austen." He followed this by begging me to remain on for a few days and go wild-pig hunting with him in the mountains.

The gendarme officer was a curious specimen as well, a little ball of a man who had the habit of stroking his mustache or blowing through pursed lips as if he found the world ridiculous. There was the mannered weariness of an old roué, yet his eyes were sharp and tough, and I had the feeling that he was an excellent shot. Once when I was leaning toward the khan and listening with perhaps more solemnness than necessary, he, as if to chide me, bent down and with the end of his cigarette holder tickled the sole of my foot.

The khan and his guests talked, as Iranians often do, of poetry, politics, and sex. The gendarme officer told the story of a peasant girl who, gathering wood in the mountains, was ravished by a bear. The doctor, laughing deeply, said that it was probably no worse for the girl than if she had been taken by an old animal like himself. We talked also of the fact, shocking to them, that I in my forties was still unmarried. What, the khan wanted to know, did I think of tribal women and should he make a match for me. I thought of those oval, strong-featured faces, vivid with the health of constant movement in the open air, of their straight, full bodies and graceful, swinging walks, and I told him, as I sincerely believed, that I thought them among the most splendid women on earth. What then would I give for a girl? Silver money? Sheep? Guns, of course, would be the best. I told him that I could only give myself, and since I was neither young, handsome, nor strong, there was not much of value in that. He protested politely: I was a fine figure of a man. But as though embarrassed by his lie, he left it quickly and went on to what he said was the only real obstacle to a match. I would put the girl in a house, and except for excursions to the baths and mosque she would live there cooped up all her life.

The gendarme officer blew hard through his pursed lips. Then he leaned forward and, shaking the cigarette holder like a scolding finger, explained that in the khan's judgement it was criminal to live in a house, to pay taxes, to be at peace with one's neighbors, and in general to lead a quiet, useful life. The gendarme officer blew again, leaned back, and closed his eyes. He opened them again, narrowed, when the khan replied. No, the khan did not believe that the settled life was criminal, but there was of course no question that it turned a man to pulp. With that he seemed to dismiss the subject, but then a sudden, violent start came into his eyes and he turned his face away from us. Something strange had come into the atmosphere, strange and frightening like the stillness that portends the rising of a terrible wind. No one moved or spoke. Then what had risen subsided, and the khan once again became our host.

He asked the doctor to give us a poem, and the doctor, delighted, cleared his throat and began to recite a long love ballad. They gave their perfect attention, as Iranians do to poetry, believing it to be the medium of truth. Only once was there a movement. Nemat, standing as straight as a palace guard, refusing out of deference to sit before the khan, noticed that the khan's prayer beads lay on the carpet a little beyond his reach. Quickly he knelt, picked up the beads, and then, after holding them out in cupped hands to the khan, retreated, walking backward, as one does before a king.

When the doctor had finished his poem, dinner was brought in. The servants laid a long cloth on the carpet and set down the heavy copper trays of food. There were chickens in mounds of saffron-sprinkled rice, goat cheese mixed with tarragon and parsley, pickled mountain celery, stacks of unleavened bread, and big pitchers of yogurt water flavored with mint.

We ate without speaking much. Halfway through, a shepherd with a bamboo flute sat down at the edge of the room and played for us, his body bending to the melody as though it were a lover. The gendarme officer grunted now and then in enjoyment of his food, and once the doctor, kissing the tips of his greasy fingers, bowed to the khan. As we each finished, we moved back against the bolsters and, resting in our fullness, looked out at the night, the distant dim line of the mountains, and the cypresses rising tapered and black, like giant pointers showing us the stars. The gendarme officer hummed a little to himself, and the doctor began a story. Then, suddenly, there was a hush in the air, and we were quiet, for snow had begun to fall, slowly and gently, like a curtain across the open arch.

It was time to sleep, and I got up to go. But the khan put his hand on my arm and said that it was out of the question for me to stay at the teahouse. I must remain on as his guest, but he was sorry that his present guest quarters were so poor. If I had been with him at a usual time, I would have had a black tent laid with his best carpets and, to honor me, a pennant on a staff placed before my door.

A staircase in the corner of the courtyard brought us into a small penthouse, which was mattressed from wall to wall and covered with eiderdowns. We undressed and snuggled down into our enormous bed. The gendarme officer moaned a little before falling asleep. The doctor tossed his great hulk back and forth and then finally began to snore. For a little while I lay awake looking out through the windows at the village below, at rest beneath the falling snow.

The next morning we went with the two tribesmen to the valley above the village to get the wood. It was a small place, a wedge of sharp green meadowland between flinty, grey foothills. At the end of the wedge, out of a tumble of boulders, came a stream. It pooled there, and then zigzagged down through the center of the meadow. Our trees stood to either side of it.

It was hot working in the sun. Soon all of us were in our shirt sleeves. Nemat rolled his high to show off the bulge of his muscles. And indeed, he wielded the ax with unflagging force. Once, panting with fatigue, I stopped and looked at him. "I am never tired," he said.

At midmorning we stopped for tea made with melted snow because the tribesmen said that with snow-water it was better. Then we smoked and skimmed stones across the stream, and the tribesmen told us hunting stories. Presently Nemat stood up, stretched, and said that though it wasn't really necessary he was going to go and make water because the place was so open and fresh.

By early afternoon we had filled the back of the Land-rover and had piled up another stack to be brought down later by a local truck. When we were ready to leave, the khan came to bid us goodbye. He thanked us for coming and told us that next year we must visit earlier so that we might see his people, how beautiful his women were, how strong his men. Then he gave me his gift: a saddlebag made of tribal cloth, harsh stuff but with a design of much delicacy woven into it. As we drove off, I turned back and saw him standing there where the valley narrowed, his feet planted a little apart, as another man might stand in the doorway of his house.

I never went back to Dehkuh even though the government later paved the road — the better, I suppose, to get troops and gendarmes in and make it safe. Not long after our trip, Nemat disappeared, going — some people thought — to his mother's people, the tribe. The doctor I saw only once again, at the hotel in town. Somehow he wasn't quite his old flamboyant self; the brocaded necktie and the heavy scent of roses were gone, nor was there any mention of wild-pig hunting in the mountains. He told me that the gendarme officer had been transferred to an office in some town and that the khan was dead. He did not know, nor did I ever learn, the circumstances, except that it was connected in some way with guns. They are needed in tribal life for hunting and the protection of flocks, but they can and have been used for other purposes as well — brigandage, for example, and revolt. In that last year the government stepped up its program of disarming the tribes. He resisted.

We mixed the wood with our local stuff to make it go further, for I hated to see the end of it. Often on those winter nights it seemed to me that it burned brighter than the rest, and remembering the khan saying that it made fine rifle stocks, I would watch it, there behind my walls, giving up its fierceness and its light, becoming ash.

Epilogue

The Development

ONE AFTERNOON in a spring of the early seventies, the merchant from whom I leased the farm stepped through the gate with a tape measure in his hand. He did not, as usual, call at the house, but went down to the cypress alley. Mamdali came to tell me this, and so I went down after him to find out what was up.

When we met in the cypress alley, he looked everywhere except at me, like a little boy caught out. Then he gathered himself together and said, "Dear gentleman, forgive me for not calling at the house. But you see I am so excited! I have such plans. As you know, our poor town has no suburb, unlike your fine towns in America." He came closer to me, his eyes staring, though not at me but at some vision. "And now I am going to make one!"

"What?" I said, not comprehending, or anyway not wanting to.

"Here," he said, his arms sweeping the alley and the orchard. "You see, the road is paved now and now, too, every day more of our people are getting cars from the new factories in Tehran. Of course, it's a little early for what I want to do, it will be a few years yet but," he bowed in apology, "I have always been ahead of my time; that is how I have made my money. So —" and his arm again swept the alley and the orchard, "I shall subdivide."

He must have seen the look on my face and he was a

kindly man. Putting his hand on my arm, he said, "But you must not worry, dear sir. You may stay here as long as you wish. I will leave you the big house and the lawn — down to the walnut. The rest — well, I have in mind lots of two hundred by two hundred."

I suppose the look on my face had not changed, for he grew more distressed. "Come," he said, taking my arm. "Let's walk a little. I understand. Living in that old house in the midst of all the fine new villas, you will, of course, lose face. I know; I understand." He stopped and turned to me, smiling. "And I have an idea for that. Go into town for a few months and I will tear down the old house and build you in its place the finest villa of them all, steel windows, a furnace —," he paused, searching for the word, for we were speaking in English, "— and plumbing, oh such plumbing, and in a pastel color!"

The next day I had business in the town. When I got back, Mamdali was waiting at the gate. "Come," he said. We went down the cypress alley to the millstone table, that fine old round of speckled stone which we had put there with a bench because it was the best view in the Garden, across the vineyards to the mountains. The stone and bench were there as ever, but the pomegranate that had bowered them was gone, for at right angles to the alley they had chopped down a swath of trees right across to the south wall of the farm. It was to be, Mamdali said, one of the roads of the subdivision.

I went back to the house and wrote out a note and a telegram: the note to the carpenter who had been the Prince's friend, telling him to come as soon as he was free to pack me up; the telegram to my friends in Tehran, asking for the loan of Akbari the jester, thinking I would need him.

A few days later, the carpenter, his apprentice, and Akbari all arrived together. As they stood there in the study doorway, I caught their first anxious, scrutinizing glances, for they knew me well enough to know that leaving the Garden would be hard for me. But in an instant the scrutiny disappeared and they went into their act: how happy they were to hear of my good fortune, the reunion with my family, the pleasures of the journey back, and all the many comforts and conveniences I would enjoy again in America. All the time they watched, trying to gauge their success in getting me to put a good face on the whole affair. I went along with them, touched by their intent. When they saw this, assured that there was now a base of cheerfulness, however forced, they permitted themselves a little truth.

"You'll miss the fruit," the carpenter said, "fine fruit in this Garden. And this house, it's old but —," he pounded the wall. "I understand that in America they build high but thin." And he pounded the five-foot wall again.

Akbari, a skull's grin on his forlorn old face, pointed out, in his usual fashion, the good and bad of what was to happen. "You are very lucky, for now you'll be rid of us terrible Iranians, every one of us crooked as a snake. They say the Americans are honest." He wrinkled his nose. "I hope that doesn't make them flat."

But it was Mamdali who brought together the two things that were going on, the grief and the necessity of facing it, and blended them into a mood which gave due regard to each, the old Iranian acceptance of fate. "Nothing lasts," he said. "Neither this Garden, nor ourselves, nor anything else. God wishes it."

The packing took some time. Akbari was forever asking us to join him in his opium and we often did. Then there was the fact that the carpenter enjoyed problems and their slow, methodical solution. I see him now, holding an object of the wrong size and shape for the space left in the crate. He would stroke his jaw, looking at the object and the crate, and then slowly and with much care, like a man making a crucial move in chess, begin to rearrange the crate. Also, he took much time in wrapping each object. First its dimensions and the degree of its fragility were noted. Then the object was simply looked at for itself. If it was in some way interesting or beautiful, he would hold it at arm's length and gaze at it for a moment. In the case of those objects that received his particular approbation, he would call the apprentice. "Here, boy; look at this. How beautiful!"

Mamdali was also very slow in wrapping things because for him almost every object in the house had its associations. If these associations were strong, he would look down at the object with tilted head and utter "eh eh." This "eh eh" had always been his habit when he was reminded of some happening or person, sad or happy, "with sin" or "with grace," that had left for the past. When it came time to pack the vodka decanter, the string of "eh"s was very long. He also believed that certain objects deserved special wrapping. On taking down my father's photograph from its place above the ranks of other photographs on the study wall, he insisted on unpacking a whole crate to get at a fine piece of old brocade, for it was in this, he believed, that the photograph should be wrapped.

The evenings were the best times. The furniture had been removed from the study some time before, so we would sit there on carpets by the fire as, in his day, old Salar Jang had done. There was much talk of the past, people and places that all of us had known. But there was also much ribbing and joking plus the tales and shadow plays of Akbari — all of which they seemed to administer as a doctor might administer a dose, feeling, I suppose, that I should not be allowed to lapse into depression.

When the packing was finally finished, Mamdali arranged a little party to be held at the *bonigah*. He borrowed a samovar, brought pastries from the town, and laid the place with carpets. Among the friends and neighbors invited, and in addition to the carpenter and Akbari, there were Mr. Dadgah and Mr. Bazargan; Aqa Ahmad, the Prince's old secretary; the miller; and Jahan Shah. Mamdali's cousin, the shoemaker, was absent, for as usual he was off on pilgrimage. But Gholam Ali, the scoundrel from the village where I had seen the passion play, was there, for we had sold him the Arab mare and he had come that day to pick her up. Finally, and for old times' sake, Ali the gardener was with us. And following the Iranian dictum that in the end all things should be forgiven, we gave him back his title and called him Ra'is.

It was a quiet gathering, for Iranians have a perfect sense of occasion, of the mood suitable to each, and for this one, which signified an ending, they blended sadness, dignity, and gentleness. With the vodka brought by Mr. Bazargan there were some toasts. Mr. Dadgah, a sad smile on his old owl's face, raised his glass to "our exploits in the field." Jahan Shah drank deeply to Fatima, and the carpenter remembered our dead Prince. Then, standing and bowing, they drank to me and Mamdali.

We stayed on for a little while with Mamdali's tea and cakes. Akbari and the miller exchanged their gloomy reflections on the condition of the planet. Gholam Ali offered me one of his wristwatches and queried the possibility of a job in the States. Mr. Dadgah and Aqa Ahmad discussed the terrible legal battle being waged by the half-brothers over the Prince's estate. As for Ra'is Ali, he told me that in forgiving him I had become a "true Iranian."

Finally, Jahan Shah proposed another round of drinks.

"No," said Mr. Dadgah, "it would not be suitable to rois-
ter." With that he raised his great bottom from the carpet
and raised his hat, and we knew that our gathering was
over. Slowly we walked together up the cypress alley to
the gate and there wished one another good fortune and
pledged that we would not forget our times together.
And we have not.

The next day the truck arrived to take my things and
Mamdali's to the town for shipment — mine to go to a
port on the gulf, Mamdali's back to his village in the east.
A little while before the truck came, we took our last walk
in the Garden, stopping at the walnut, the millstone, the
bonigah, and in the cypress alley. Then I went into the
house and walked through the empty rooms, their emptiness filling with memories of people and of times. Finally, I stood beneath the key vault and saluted it, for I
knew that in a few days the landlord's men would come to
lay the dynamite.

When the truck came, I walked out to the gate. This
time the usual little ceremony did not take place. In the
past, when I had left for brief visits to Europe or the
States, Khanom would wait for me to pass through the
gate and then pour water on the dust of the threshold I
had crossed. I never thought to ask her the significance
of this, but I suppose the dust was my departure; the
water, my return. This time there was only the dust.

Outside the gate we stood for a moment gazing at one
another, and in that moment, like a drowning man, I saw
our past together. While I stood there looking back at it,
Mamdali came up and kissed me on both cheeks, Khanom
took my hand between her own, and the children nestled
at my side. Then in their last kindness, and saving me the
act, they went and closed the gates of the Garden for
good.